The Buddhism
of Tibet
and
The Key to
the Middle Way

THE WISDOM OF TIBET SERIES

By Nāgārjuna and the Seventh Dalai Lama

The Precious Garland
and
The Song of the Four Mindfulnesses

volume 2

The Buddhism of Tibet and The Key to the Middle Way

TENZIN GYATSO
The Fourteenth Dalai Lama

Translated in the main by
Jeffrey Hopkins and Lati Rimpoche

London   George Allen & Unwin Ltd
Ruskin House   Museum Street

First published in 1975

This translation © George Allen & Unwin Ltd. 1975

ISBN 0 04 294086 9 hardback
ISBN 0 04 294087 7 paperback

Library of Congress form of author's name:
Bstan-'dzin-rgya-mtsho, Dalai Lama XIV, 1935–

Printed in Great Britain
in 12 point Fournier type
by Unwin Brothers Limited
The Gresham Press
Old Woking Surrey

*Published under the aegis of
the Library of Tibetan Works and Archives
with the authority of
His Holiness the Dalai Lama
as revealing oral tradition*

Foreword

Sentient beings in general and mankind in particular have made and are continuing to make efforts to bring about their happiness and comfort by many different methods in accordance with their varying abilities. However, through a multitude of bad causes, both external and internal, they are continually tormented by many sufferings such as mental agitation and so forth. People in particular, unlike other living beings, create disturbances for themselves and others by reason of differences such as of country, race, political system and theory. As a result of these differences, groups of men are amassed, war is made and so on. Like intentionally putting a finger in its own eye, mankind consciously engages in many techniques that bring various undesirable consequences upon itself, such as causes for fear, man-made diseases, starvation and untimely death.

I have thought that under the circumstances of such a delicate time as described above, it would be wonderful if even a few people for a short period could have some internal peace. Also, many intelligent persons are analysing and seeking the meaning of emptiness. Based on that, I have commissioned the translation into English and publication of the following works:

The Buddhism of Tibet and *The Key to the Middle Way*, both by myself.
The Precious Garland of Advice for the King, by the protector Nāgārjuna. This good explanation is a great compendium of both the profound emptiness and the extensive deeds of compassion, illuminating as well techniques for social welfare.
The Song of the Four Mindfulnesses, by Kaysang Gyatso, the Seventh Dalai Lama. This work has only a few words, but contains all the essentials of sūtra and tantra.

9

The present volume contains my own works. The two texts by Nāgārjuna and Kaysang Gyatso form the second volume in this series.

The Buddhist monk, Tenzin Gyatso, BE 2516, AD 1972, the Tibetan Water Mouse year in the tenth month on the twelfth day.

Contents

I
The Buddhism of Tibet

TENZIN GYATSO
The Fourteenth Dalai Lama

Translated by Jeffrey Hopkins
with Anne Klein

Preface

This introduction to Tibetan Buddhism is intended for beginners. The first half is a revised version of the appendix called *An Outline of Buddhism in Tibet* in my book *My Land and My People*. The second half expounds briefly the significance of the refuge, the concordance of actions and their fruits, the three trainings and Bodhicitta.

May those who seek the path of peace and happiness find it.

The Buddhist monk Tenzin Gyatso
(*The Fourteenth Dalai Lama*)

The Need for Religious Practice in Our Present Lives

The reason why we should engage in religious practice is that no matter how much material progress there is, it alone cannot generate adequate and lasting pleasure. Indeed, the more we progress materially, the more we have to live in constant fear and anxiety. Through progress in new fields of knowledge we have reached the moon, which some ancient peoples regarded as a source of refuge. Although there may be instances where the resources of the moon and other planets can be utilised for the advantage of human beings, perhaps in the end such advances will make enemies outside our world. In any case, such techniques can never bring ultimate and lasting happiness to human beings. These methods induce only an external physical pleasure; therefore, even though slight mental pleasure sometimes arises due to these conditions, it cannot last. On the other hand, it is widely known that when one searches for happiness in terms only of the mind, physical hardships are easy to bear. This depends on engaging in the practice of religious methods and transforming the mind.

Furthermore, even the arising of pleasure in this life depends on religious practice. Pleasure and pain, whether great or small, do not arise from superficial external factors alone; one must have their internal causes. These are the potencies or latencies of virtuous and non-virtuous actions in the mind. These potencies are in a dormant state; they are activated when one encounters external causes, and thus feelings of pleasure or pain occur. If these potencies are absent, no matter how many external factors are present, there is no way for pleasure or pain to appear or disappear. Such potencies are established by deeds done in the past.

Therefore, regardless of what form of suffering the effect takes, one initially must have done a bad deed through an undisciplined mind and thereby 'accumulated' such a deed. The deed's potency is established in the mind, and later, when one meets with certain causes, suffering is undergone. Thus, all pleasures and pains basically derive from the mind. For this reason, the mind cannot be disciplined without religious practice, and by not disciplining the mind bad actions are 'accumulated'. They in turn establish potencies in one's mental continuum, in dependence on which the fruits of suffering are produced.

The Need for Religious Practice for Our Future Lives

Although in some regions of existence beings have only minds, most sentient beings also have a physical base. Both body and mind have their direct causes, and if we illustrate this with birth from a womb, the direct cause of the body is the semen of the father and the blood of the mother. The mind likewise has a direct cause of a type similar to itself. The beginning in this life of the continuum of the mind that is of similar type to the present mind is the mind at the moment of its 'linking' to the centre of the mingled semen and blood of the parents. This mental entity must definitely have a former continuum, because external phenomena cannot become mind and mind cannot become external phenomena. If a continuum of this mental entity necessarily exists, then it definitely must be a mind before its 'linking' [to the new life]. This establishes the existence of a former life.

Because such a mind is one continuum, even nowadays there are cases of former lives being remembered by some adults and children who have all the conditions conducive to such memory. In attested biographies from the past there are also many instances of remembrance of former lives.

Although cause and effect are different, they must be related through partial similarity. For example, because a body has tangibility, shape, and colour, its direct cause must also have these qualities; and because a mind does not have shape and so forth, its direct cause cannot have these qualities either. Analogously, seeds of sweet-tasting plants create fruits that are sweet. Therefore, the parents' semen and blood, which are physical, cannot be put as the direct cause of a non-physical mind. In dependence on this and other reasons, it can definitely be concluded that former and later lives exist. Then, as former and later lives do exist, it is extremely clear that there is nothing except religious practice that is helpful for the continuum of lives. These are the reasons why religious practice is necessary.

Buddhism, One of the Many Religions of the World: Its Teacher

In this world, just as there are many medicines for a particular disease, so there are many religious systems that serve as methods for achieving happiness for all sentient beings, human and otherwise. Though each of these systems has different modes of practice and different modes of expression, I think that they are all similar in that they improve the body, speech and mind of those who practise them, and in that they all have good aims. They are all similar in teaching that bad actions of speech, such as lying and divisiveness, and bad physical actions, such as stealing and killing, are improper.

It is sad that throughout history there have been instances of struggle and hatred among the followers of different religions. It would be good if these were all things in the past that would never happen again. The practitioners of religions definitely could come to agree together. At present there are, in general, the two factions of those who do and those who do not engage in religious practice; it is therefore important that practitioners be unified without bias. This is not to be done with a sense of hatred [for those who do not practise]. Not only will unity help practitioners, but also its very purpose should be to achieve temporary and lasting help and happiness for non-practitioners as well. It would serve as a method for removing their ignorance, which obscures what should be adopted and what should be discarded, and would set them on a path towards ultimate happiness. I wish to offer my hopes and prayers that all religions unite to achieve this purpose.

Books written or translated in the past have certainly done a great service to Buddhism, but some of them, other than giving only a rough treatment of the path, cannot provide the deeper significance. To remedy this situation a cultural institution called the Library of Tibetan Works and Archives has been established. Among other activities, it has undertaken the translation into English of several works from original Tibetan sources. Translation teams consisting of Tibetan and foreign scholars have been specially set up for this purpose. The present volume forms the first in the series of this project of producing translations that accord with the oral tradition and the real meaning of all the technical terms. For followers of religious systems to come together, they must be able to know and understand each other's systems, and to this end I am presenting a brief introduction to the Buddhism of Tibet.

Our teacher, Śākyamuni Buddha, is one among the thousand

Buddhas of this aeon. These Buddhas were not Buddhas from the beginning, but were once sentient beings like ourselves. How they came to be Buddhas is this. Of body and mind, mind is predominant, for body and speech are under the influence of the mind. Afflictions such as desire do not contaminate the nature of the mind, for the nature of the mind is pure, uncontaminated by any taint. Afflictions are peripheral factors of a mind, and through gradually transforming all types of defects, such as these afflictions, the adventitious taints can be completely removed. This state of complete purification is Buddhahood; therefore, Buddhists do not assert that there is any Buddha who has been enlightened from the beginning.

Buddhas are always striving for the welfare of beings migrating in cyclic existence. In every hour and minute they create limitless forms of welfare for beings through billions of emanations of their body, speech and mind. For instance, in this aeon—an aeon being a period of an extremely great number of years—they will appear in the aspect of one thousand supreme Emanation Bodies (Nirmāṇakāya) as Buddhas, and each will have his own new teaching.

The teaching of Śākyamuni Buddha is different from the teachings of the other Buddhas in that his has a union of sūtra and tantra, whereas most of the others do not have any tantra. [Śākyamuni Buddha was actually enlightened many aeons ago, but] from the point of view of common appearances his life was a display of twelve main events: his descent from the Joyous Pure Land (Tuṣita), his conception, birth, schooling, mastery in the arts, sporting with his retinue of wives, renunciation, asceticism, meditation under the tree of enlightenment, conquest of the array of evil ones, becoming a Buddha, turning the wheel of doctrine, and nirvāṇa.

Buddha's coming to this world was for the sake of beings migrating in cyclic existence. Because his miraculous exhibition of speech is chief among the three types of miraculous exhibitions [body, speech and mind], his coming was for the sake of turning the wheel of doctrine.

The teacher Śākyamuni was born in a royal family, and in the early part of his life he performed his princely duties. When he saw that all the marvels of cyclic existence are of the nature of suffering, he renounced his kingdom and began to practise asceticism. Finally, at Bodh Gayā, he displayed the ways of becoming fully enlightened. Then in stages he turned the three renowned wheels of doctrine.

In the first period, at Varaṇāsī, Buddha turned the wheel of doctrine that is based on the four noble truths; he did this mainly in consideration of those having the lineage of Hearers (Śrāvaka). In the middle period, at Gṛdhrakūṭa, he set forth the middle wheel of doctrine, which is based on the mode of non-inherent existence of all phenomena; he did this mainly in consideration of trainees of sharp faculties who bear the Mahāyāna lineage. In the final period, at Vaiśālī, he set forth the final wheel [which is based on discriminating between those phenomena that do and those that do not truly exist]; he did this mainly in consideration of trainees of middling and lower faculties who bear the Mahāyāna lineage. The teacher Buddha also appeared in the body of Vajradhara and set forth tantric doctrines.

The volumes of translations into Tibetan that are widely known nowadays as the Kangyur are solely the word of Buddha. The sūtra portion of the Blessed One's word is incorporated in the three scriptural divisions. These are arranged according to their subject matter: the discipline (vinaya) is concerned with ethics (śīla); the class of scripture (sūtrānta) with meditative stabilisation (samādhi); and knowledge (abhidharma) with wisdom (prajñā). The tantric doctrines are incorporated in the four sets of tantra. Or, in another way, the four sets of tantra can be included in the scriptural division called 'class of scripture'.

The Spread of Buddhism to Tibet

Long before Buddhism spread to Tibet the Bon religion, which came from the country of Shang-Shung, was prevalent in Tibet, and even nowadays there are lecturers and practitioners of the Bon system. Originally, it seems not to have been very extensive in scope. However, when later the Buddhist teaching spread from India and was widely disseminated in Tibet, it appears that the Bon system of assertion on view, meditation and behaviour became more vast and profound.

The Buddhist teaching first spread to Tibet during the reign of the Tibetan King Hla-to-to-ri-nyen-tsen (Lha-tho-tho-ri-gnyan-bstan). Then it gradually increased, and many famous Indian scholars, such as Śāntarakṣita and Kamalaśīla, as well as many adepts, such as Padmasaṃbhava, translated and disseminated many sūtras, tantras and commentaries. During the reign of Lang-dar-ma (gLang-dar-ma), the teaching suffered a setback for almost a decade, but revived again, starting from the eastern and western parts of Tibet. This marked the beginning of the later dissemination of Buddhism in Tibet. Many scholars, such as Rin-chen-sang-po (Rin-chen-bzang-po), met with famous Indian scholars and adepts and through hearing, thinking and meditating maintained and furthered the Conqueror's teaching. Also, many Indian scholars, such as Atiśa, came to Tibet and translated and disseminated many sūtras, tantras and commentaries. At this point, many of Tibet's own people became skilled in the doctrine and began writing the many Tibetan commentaries, and after a time not many famous Indian or Nepalese scholars came to Tibet.

Thus, the Buddhist teaching that spread to Tibet is just the stainless teaching of India and nothing else. The Tibetan lamas neither altered it nor mixed it with another religion. For example, in Tibetan commentaries, even after a brief exegesis of doctrine, a source is cited, be it the speech of Buddha himself or of another Indian scholar, and the point is settled only on this basis. As an extremely clear proof, during detailed discussions I have had with modern Indian scholars of both Buddhist and non-Buddhist philosophies they have said that even in instances where it is difficult to understand the meaning of doctrinal passages, the entire meaning is given in the Tibetan translations done many centuries ago. Not only that, but also some Indians scholars say that some passages which are difficult to understand in Sanskrit are understood more easily through looking at the Tibetan translations. On the basis of this information I think that those who, noticing the slight differences with Indian Buddhism due to locality, time, or external conditions, identify Tibetan Buddhism as 'Lamaism' specifically in the sense of its being a transformation of Buddhism are completely wrong. Also, at the present time, if one wants to know thoroughly all the views, meditations and practices of Hīnayāna and Mahāyāna, I think that one should read the Tibetan treatises with fine analysis over a long period of time. I may be wrong, so I hope that no one will take offence.

In India formerly, even though the systems of explanation of the scholars at Nālanda and those at Vikramaśīla were essentially the same, there were slight differences in their names and modes of instruction. In the same way, different names arose in Tibet due to the names of the lineages of Indian scholars and their students, localities, times and so forth; the more famous of these schools are the Nying-ma (rNying-ma), Ka-gyü (bKa'-rgyud), Sa-kya (Sa-skya) and Ge-luk (dGe-lugs). Though they are fundamentally the same, they have several differences in mode of instruction. Still, all of them are only the Conqueror's teaching of a union of sūtra and tantra.

The Meaning of *Dharma*

The word *dharma* in Sanskrit means 'that which holds'. All existents are *dharmas*, phenomena, in the sense that they hold or bear their own entity or character. Also, a religion is a *dharma* in the sense that it holds persons back or protects them from disasters. Here the term *dharma* refers to the latter definition. In rough terms, any elevated action of body, speech or mind is regarded as a *dharma* because through doing such an action one is protected or held back from all sorts of disasters. Practice of such actions is practice of *dharma*. Since this is not the time to deal at length with the topic of *dharma*, only the Buddhist *dharma* will be explained briefly here in comprehensible terms.

The Four Noble Truths

The Blessed One said, 'These are true sufferings, these are true sources, these are true cessations, these are true paths. Sufferings are to be known, their sources are to be abandoned, their cessations are to be actualised, the paths are to be cultivated. Sufferings are to be known; then, there will be no more suffering to be known. The sources of sufferings are to be abandoned; then, there will be no more sources to be abandoned. The cessations of suffering are to be actualised; then, there will be no more cessations to be actualised. The paths are to be cultivated; then, there will be no more paths to be cultivated.' These are the four noble truths in terms of their entities, requisite actions, and actions together with their effects. In explaining them, the interpretation of the Prāsaṅgika-Mādhyamika system, the highest among all Buddhist schools, will mainly be followed.

True sufferings are phenomena that arise from contaminated actions and afflictions and that are included within the term 'cyclic existence'. True sources are the causes producing true sufferings. True cessations are the states of extinguishment and disappearance of true sufferings and true sources. True paths are special methods for attaining true cessations.

Because true sufferings arise from true sources, true sources actually precede true sufferings. Also, through cultivating true paths, true cessations are actualised; true paths therefore, actually precede true cessations. However, the Blessed One reversed this order when he taught the four noble truths, and this is extremely important. For, if initially one recognises the sufferings, then one investigates their causes; therefore, Buddha set forth the sources of suffering after identifying the sufferings themselves. When one generates confidence in the ability to eliminate these sources, then a wish to actualise their cessation arises. Then for the sake of doing this, a wish to cultivate the paths arises; therefore, Buddha set forth the true paths after identifying true cessations.

Cyclic Existence and Sentient Beings

One might wonder, 'Since cyclic existence together with its miseries are true sufferings, what is cyclic existence?'

Cyclic existence is divided into three types by way of different types of abodes; these are a desire realm, a form realm and a formless realm. In the desire realm, beings partake of the pleasures of the 'five desirous attributes': forms, sounds, odours, tastes and tangible objects. The form realm has two parts: in the lower, beings are not attracted to external pleasures but partake of the pleasures of internal contemplation. In the higher part, beings have turned away from pleasurable feelings altogether and partake of neutral feelings. In the formless realm all forms, sounds, odours, tastes and tangible objects and the five senses for enjoying them are absent; there is only mind, and beings abide only in neutral feeling, one-pointedly and without distraction.

There are six different types of sentient beings who migrate in cyclic existence: gods, demigods, humans, hungry ghosts, animals and denizens of hells. Gods include beings in the form and formless realms as well as the six types of gods in the desire realm. Demigods are similar to gods but are mischievous and rough. Humans are those of the four 'continents' and so forth. Hungry ghosts are many types of beings who are severely deprived of food and drink. Animals are those in the ocean and those scattered about the surface of the earth. Denizens of hells are persons born in various colours and shapes through the force of and in accordance with their own previous actions.

The essential meaning of 'cyclic existence' is a process outside of one's control, that proceeds in accordance with contaminated actions and afflictions. Its essential nature is misery; its function is to provide a basis for suffering and to induce suffering in the future. Technically, cyclic existence is the contaminated mental and physical aggregates appropriated through contaminated actions and afflictions. Because there is nothing in all three realms to which cyclic existence does not apply, the mental and physical aggregates of all these beings are cyclic existences.

Causes of Cyclic Existence

What are the roots of cyclic existence? The sources of suffering are two: contaminated actions and afflictions.

Afflictions are classed as peripheral mental factors and are not themselves any of the six main minds [eye, ear, nose, tongue, body and mental consciousnesses]. However, when any of the afflicting mental factors becomes manifest, a main mind [a mental consciousness] comes under its influence, goes wherever the affliction leads it, and 'accumulates' a bad action.

There are a great many different kinds of afflictions, but the chief of them are desire, hatred, pride, wrong view and so forth. Of these, desire and hatred are chief. Because of an initial attachment to oneself, hatred arises when something undesirable occurs. Further, through being attached to oneself the pride that holds one to be superior arises, and similarly when one has no knowledge of something, a wrong view that holds the object of this knowledge to be non-existent arises.

How do self-attachment and so forth arise in such great force? Because of beginningless conditioning, the mind tightly holds to 'I, I' even in dreams, and through the power of this conception, self-attachment and so forth occur. This false conception of 'I' arises because of one's lack of knowledge concerning the mode of existence of things. The fact that all objects are empty of inherent existence is obscured and one conceives things to exist inherently; the strong conception of 'I' derives from this. Therefore, the conception that phenomena inherently exist is the afflicting ignorance that is the ultimate root of all afflictions.

Actions

From the point of view of their nature, actions are of two types: intentional and operational. An intentional action occurs prior to physical or verbal deeds and is a mental factor that provides the impulse to act. An operational action is a physical or verbal action that occurs at the time of engaging in activity.

From the point of view of the effects they impel, actions are of three types: meritorious, non-meritorious and invariable. Meritorious actions impel one to happy migrations, which are the lives of humans, demigods and gods. Non-meritorious actions impel one to bad migrations, which are the lives of animals, hungry ghosts and denizens of hells. Invariable actions impel one to the upper realms, which are those of form and the formless.

All of these can be divided into physical, verbal and mental actions. Also, from the point of view of how the effects are experienced, actions can be divided into three types: the effects of an action 'accumulated' in this life may be experienced in this very life, in the next life, or in any life beyond the next.

Liberation

Cyclic existence means bondage, and liberation means freedom from this bondage. As was explained above, the causes of cyclic existence are contaminated actions and afflictions. If the roots of the afflictions are eliminated and if new actions are not 'accumulated', since there are no afflictions to activate the predispositions of contaminated actions persisting from the past, the causes of cyclic existence have been eliminated. Then there is freedom from bondage. Some say that as long as one still has mental and physical aggregates wrought by former contaminated actions and afflictions one has a nirvāṇa with remainder. When these no longer remain, there is a nirvāṇa without remainder. 'Without remainder' means that there is no remainder of mental and physical aggregates wrought by contaminated actions and afflictions, but the continuum of consciousness and the continuum of uncontaminated mental and physical aggregates still exist.

Through removing the cause, the contaminated aggregates

cease, and through becoming free from them all, the suffering that depends on them is extinguished. Such is liberation, of which there are two types: a liberation that is a mere extinguishing of sufferings and their sources and the great, unsurpassed liberation, the rank of Buddhahood. The former is an extinguishment of all the afflicting obstructions [which prevent liberation from cyclic existence] but not of the obstructions to direct cognition of all objects of knowledge. The latter liberation is the ultimate rank, an utter extinguishing of both the afflictions and the obstructions to omniscience.

Hīnayāna

In order to attain either of these liberations, one must rely on a path. There are paths of ordinary beings and paths of Superiors. The latter are true paths. There are two types of Hīnayānists: Hearers (Śrāvaka) and Solitary Realisers (Pratyekabuddha). Each of them has five paths, and thus there are ten Hīnayāna paths.

Although Hearers are lower and Solitary Realisers are higher, their basis is the same. They both practise the Hīnayāna doctrine of a path that serves as a method for achieving a mere liberation from cyclic existence for their own sakes. In brief, they take as their basis a set of ethics in conjunction with a thought definitely to get out of cyclic existence. On the basis of this, they cultivate a union of calm abiding (śamatha) and special insight (vipaśyanā), which is directed toward emptiness, and thereby extricate the afflictions together with their seeds so that it is impossible for them ever to grow again. Doing this, they attain liberation.

Both Hearers and Solitary Realisers have a series of five paths: the paths of accumulation, preparation, seeing, meditation and no more learning. One who trains in such paths is called a Hīnayānist.

THE BUDDHISM OF TIBET

Mahāyāna

Mahāyānists primarily seek the rank of Buddhahood, the non-abiding nirvāṇa, the supreme liberation, for the sake of others. In conjunction with this aspiration to highest enlightenment for the sake of all sentient beings, they practise the paths that were explained above for the Hīnayāna. However, these paths are higher and more powerful because of the difference in motivation. The paths are also augmented with special methods, the main of which are the six perfections and the four means of gathering students. Based on these, Mahāyānists overcome totally and forever not only the afflicting obstructions but also the obstructions to omniscience. When the two obstructions are overcome, they attain the rank of Buddhahood.

In the Mahāyāna there are also five paths: the Mahāyāna paths of accumulation, preparation, seeing, meditation and no more learning. Though these are similar in name to the Hīnayāna paths, they in fact have a great difference. In brief, the difference between the two vehicles of Hīnayāna and Mahāyāna lies in their initial motivation, and because of this the general body of their paths, and especially their methods or deeds, come to be different. Through this, in turn, their effects also have a great difference of inferiority and superiority.

Once Hīnayānists have attained their fruit, do they remain there? Or do they enter the Mahāyāna?

They definitely do finally enter the Mahāyāna. Because their type of liberation is not the ultimate attainment, they are not satisfied with it, but gradually seek the ultimate attainment, train in its paths and become Buddhas.

Tantrayāna

The Mantra Vehicle has four sets of tantras: Action (Kriyā),

Performance (Caryā), Yoga, and Highest Yoga (Anuttara-yoga). The Highest Yoga set of tantras is superior to the lower ones. Many tens of millions of Highest Yoga tantras were set forth, but this procedure will be dealt with only briefly.

It was explained above that the various sufferings which we experience are due to the power of contaminated actions and afflictions; essentially, sufferings arise because one has been unable to tame the mind. In Highest Yoga, the methods for taming the mind are to meditate on a salutary object within the context of not allowing bad thoughts to be generated, and along with this to concentrate on important places in the body. Through these methods the Highest Yoga path is faster than the others, and this is due to the fact that the mind depends on the body. One concentrates on the various channels in which mainly blood, mainly semen, or only currents of energy [winds] flow. Then, since currents of energy cause the mind to move to objects, a yogī reverses these currents, and thus there is nothing to stir the mind; the mind does not stir or move to other objects. These are the methods that are employed in Highest Yoga.

Since such skill comes only through internal practice involving the channels and the currents of energy and not through external factors, the mind must have a strong ability to keep on its object. For the sake of acquiring this ability as well as for other reasons, the texts teach meditation on the body of a deity and so forth. The many images of deities in tantra are not arbitrary creations; they are means of purifying the impure mental and physical aggregates (skandha), the types (dhātu) and the sources (āyatana). Also the peaceful and wrathful aspects, the numbers of faces and hands, the number of principal and surrounding figures and so forth are due to differences in the trainees' dispositions, thoughts and faculties.

In brief, although there are definitely instances of achievements among these paths through the power of belief, these paths are mostly achieved through the power of reasoning. If one trains in the paths correctly and gradually, there are many reasons one can find to facilitate the attainment of conviction and a well-founded belief.

The Two Truths

Among the paths mentioned above, the paths of Superiors are true paths; the others are as if precursors to these. All the paths are included within method and wisdom. Method and wisdom, in turn, depend on the two truths. Nāgārjuna's *Fundamental Text Called 'Wisdom'* (*Prajñā-nāma-mūla-madhyamakakārikā*, XXIV. 8) says:

> Doctrines taught by the Buddhas
> Rely wholly on the two truths,
> Conventional worldly truths
> And truths that are ultimate.

Also, the attainment of a Truth Body (Dharmakāya) and a Form Body (Rūpakāya) on the effect stage, which is Buddhahood, depends on the practice of method and wisdom while on the path. Method and wisdom, in turn, depend on the two truths which represent the mode of being of the ground or basis [of practice]. Thus, understanding the two truths is very important, and it is a very difficult topic. The many differences in the Buddhist schools of tenets are due to their different presentations of the two truths.

Let us speak here a little about the two truths in accordance with the Prāsaṅgika-Mādhyamika system. All phenomena that we manifestly perceive have two modes of being. One is the nominal or conventional entity of the phenomenon, and the other is its final mode of being, its emptiness of inherent existence. Let us give an example from another sphere; a pen, for instance, has a gross mode of being which can be seen by the ordinary eye and also has a mode of being which cannot

31

be seen by the ordinary eye and which is the fact of its being a mass of atoms.

What are the individual meanings of 'ultimate truth' and 'conventional truth?'

In rough and brief terms, an object found by a valid cogniser distinguishing a final nature is an ultimate truth and an object found by a valid cogniser distinguishing a conventionality is a conventional truth. Therefore, emptinesses and true cessations are ultimate truths, and everything else are conventional truths.

All of these phenomena have some mode of dependence; either they arise, change and cease in dependence on causes, or they are posited in dependence on a continuum, or in dependence on their parts and so forth. No matter what type of dependent phenomena they are, they exist only in dependence on another. Not even one among them is able to stand by itself. Therefore all of them are empty of their own inherent existence. Nevertheless, all agents, actions and objects are conventionally valid. In brief, because phenomena are empty of inherent existence, they change from one thing into another, and because phenomena exist conventionally, there is good and bad, and help and harm.

A General Outline of the Practice of Buddhism

The designation 'practising a religious system' is not given to mere physical change, living in a monstery, or recitation, but it still is not definite that these could not become religious practice. In any case, religious practice must be carried out in terms of one's own thought. If one knows how to bring the teachings into one's own thought, all physical and verbal deeds can be made to accord with practice. If one does not know how to bring them into one's own thought, even though one might meditate, recite scriptures, or spend one's life in a temple, it will not help; thought is therefore important for practice. Thus, taking refuge in the Three Jewels (Buddha, his Doctrine and the Spiritual Community), taking into account the relationship between actions and their effects, and generating an attitude of helping others, are most important.

Formerly in Tibet there was a famous lama called Drom. One day Drom saw a man walking around a reliquary. 'Walking around a reliquary is good,' he said. 'Practice is even better.'

The man thought, 'Then, reading a holy book would be good.' He did so, and one day while he was reading, Drom saw him and said, 'Reading a holy book is good; practice is even better.'

The man thought, 'This also does not seem to be sufficient. Now if I do some meditation, that will certainly be practice.'

Drom saw him in meditation and said, 'Meditation is good; practice is even better.' The man was amazed and asked, 'How does one practise?' Drom answered, 'Do not be attached to this life; cause your mind to become the practices.' Drom said this because practice depends on thought.

A Specific Outline of the Practice of Buddhism

There are great advantages if one renounces this life and performs the practices. In Tibet there are many people who have renounced the world and have attained an indescribable mental and physical happiness. All the pleasures that are achieved through cherishing this life and which require many types of continuous effort do not equal even a fraction of this happiness. Nevertheless, this practice is difficult for most people to undertake.

What is the mode of practice for the majority of people? In general, immoral livelihood requiring deceit, lying and so forth is the opposite of religious practice and thus is not compatible with it. However, in harmony with religious practice, one can engage in a livelihood that accords with the respectable ways of the world, such as administering a government, promoting economic measures, or taking any steps towards securing the welfare and enjoyment of others. These should be done within the context of always retaining thoughts of religious practice. It is said:

> If one practises, liberation is present even while living in a household
> As in the case of the kings and ministers of India and Tibet and others such as Marpa.
> If one does not practise, the causes of a bad migration are present even while living in a mountain retreat
> Like a woodchuck hibernating in a hole in the ground.

The Three Refuges

What are the methods for causing one's own mind to become the practices?

Initially, one should take refuge and think about actions and their effects. The refuge is the Three Jewels: Buddha, his Doctrine and the Spiritual Community.

When a sentient being purifies the taints of his own mind as well as their latent predispositions, he is free of all defects that act as obstructions. Thus, he simultaneously and directly knows all phenomena. Such a being is called a Buddha, and he is a teacher of refuge, like a physician.

The Doctrine jewel is the superior (ārya) paths—the chief right paths which remove the taints as well as their latent predispositions—and the absences which are states of having removed what is to be removed. The Doctrine is the actual refuge, like medicine.

The Community jewel is all persons, whether lay or ordained, who have generated a superior path in their continuum. They are friends helping one to achieve refuge, like nurses.

The three refuges that have been achieved and presently exist in other beings' continuums are one's own causal refuge; one relies on a protector just as a weak person takes refuge in a stronger person. The three refuges that one will attain in the future are one's own effect refuge. One who relies on the Three Jewels from the point of view of knowing that he is to attain them, must cause them to be generated in his own continuum.

Any effect, whether good or bad, must arise in dependence on causes and conditions. Thus, at present one must actually achieve in one's own continuum the causes that are similar in type to a Doctrine jewel, the actual refuge. Therefore, one must practise the paths that are included in the three trainings (triśikṣā) in higher ethics (adhiśīla), in higher meditative stabilisation (adhisamādhi), and in higher wisdom (adhiprajñā).

Training in Higher Ethics

Even though the training in ethics takes many forms, the ethics of abandoning the ten non-virtues is their basis. Of the ten non-virtues, three pertain to bodily actions, four to verbal actions and three to mental actions. The three physical non-virtues are:

1 Taking the life of a living being: ranging from killing an insect to killing a human.
2 Stealing: taking away another's property without his consent, regardless of its value, whether the deed is done by oneself or through another.
3 Sexual misconduct: committing adultery.

The four verbal non-virtues are:

4 Lying: deceiving others through spoken words or physical gestures.
5 Divisiveness: creating dissension by causing those in agreement to disagree or by causing those in disagreement to disagree even further.
6 Harshness: abusing others.
7 Senselessness: talking about foolish things motivated by desire and so forth.

The three mental non-virtues are:

8 Covetousness: thinking, 'May this become mine', desiring something that belongs to another.
9 Harmful intent: wishing to injure others, be it great or small injury.
10 Wrong view: viewing some existent thing, such as rebirth, cause and effect, or the Three Jewels, as non-existent.

The opposites of these ten non-virtues are the ten virtues, and engaging in them is called the practice of ethics.

Training in Higher Meditative Stabilisation

Then, how does one progress in the training of meditative stabilisation, which is the mind's abiding one-pointedly on its object?

There are many types of meditative stabilisation, but let us explain calm abiding (śamatha) here. The nature of calm abiding is the one-pointed abiding on any object without distraction of a mind conjoined with a bliss of physical and mental pliancy. If it is supplemented with taking refuge, it is a Buddhist practice, and if it is supplemented with an aspiration to highest enlightenment for the sake of all sentient beings, it is a Mahāyāna practice. Its merits are that, if one has achieved calm abiding, one's mind and body are pervaded by joy and bliss; one can—through the power of its mental and physical pliancy—set the mind on any virtuous object one chooses; and many special qualities such as clairvoyance and emanations are attained.

The main purpose and advantage of calm abiding are that through it one can achieve special insight (vipaśyanā), which realises emptiness, and can thereby be liberated from cyclic existence. Also, most of the secondary beneficial attributes of the three vehicles (Hīnayāna, Mahāyāna and Tantrayāna) arise in dependence on calm abiding. The benefits are many.

One should have all the following causal collections for the achievement of calm abiding. The place where one practices should be free of noise, since noise is a thorn to concentration; the area and water should be congenial. The meditator himself should have few wants, know satisfaction, be free from the din and bustle of the world, and should avoid non-virtuous physical and verbal deeds. Through hearing and thinking he should have eliminated misconceptions about the subjects of meditation, he should know how to reflect on the faults of desire, on the meaning of impermanence and so on.

With regard to the actual practice of calm abiding, Maitreya says in his *Discrimination of the Middle Way and the Extremes* (*Madhyāntavibhaṅga*):

The cause of its arising is to observe the relinquishing
Of the five faults and the application of the eight antidotes.

The five faults to be relinquished are:

1 Laziness: not wishing to cultivate meditative stabilisation.
2 Forgetfulness: not remembering the object of meditation.
3 Lethargy and excitement: interruptions of meditative stabilisation.
4 Non-application of the antidotes: occurring when lethargy and excitement arise.
5 Over-application: continuing to apply the antidotes even though lethargy and excitement have been extinguished.

The eight antidotes are the means for relinquishing these faults. The antidotes to laziness are:

1 Faith: seeing the good qualities of meditative stabilisation.
2 Aspiration: seeking to attain those good qualities.
3 Effort: delighting in engaging in meditative stabilisation.
4 Physical and mental pliancy: an effect [of effort].

The antidote to forgetfulness is:

5 Mindfulness: maintaining concentration on an object continuously.

The antidote to lethargy and excitement is:

6 Awareness: knowing that lethargy or excitement has arisen or is arising.

The antidote to non-application is:

7 Application: engaging in the antidotes to lethargy or excitement.

The antidote to over-application is:

8 Desisting from application: relaxing one's effort.

Through applying the eight antidotes the five faults are gradually eliminated, and one passes through nine states of concentration.

1 Setting the mind: collecting the mind and aiming it at an internal object [such as the visualised form of Buddha].

2 Continually setting: prolonging concentration on the object more than in the previous state.

3 Re-setting: immediately recognising distraction and returning to the object.

4 Increased setting: collecting the mind from concentrating on the gross [aspects of the visualised object of meditation] and setting it more and more steadily on the subtle [details of the object].

5 Disciplining: knowing the good qualities of meditative stabilisation and taking joy in them.

6 Pacifying: ceasing dislike for meditative stabilisation.

7 Thorough pacifying: through effort relinquishing even subtle lethargy and excitement just after they arise.

8 Making one-pointed: generating meditative stabilisation continuously within the context of its being impossible for the non-conducive to interrupt the process.

9 Putting in equipoise: spontaneously fixing on the object of meditation without requiring the effort of relying on mindfulness and awareness.

The above nine states of concentration are accomplished by means of the six powers. The first state is accomplished through the power of hearing, the second through the power of thinking, and the third and fourth through the power of mindfulness. The fifth and sixth are accomplished through the power of awareness, the seventh and eighth through the power of effort, and the ninth through the power of familiarity.

The periods of the four mental activities [which are ways in which the mind engages its object] occur during the nine states of concentration:

1 Forcibly fixing: during the first and second states the mind is strenuously fixed on its object of concentration.

39

2 Interruptedly fixing: from the third to the seventh state concentration occurs intermittently.

3 Non-interruptedly fixing: during the eighth state the mind is capable of staying on its object without interruption.

4 Effortlessly fixing: during the ninth state the mind spontaneously remains on its object.

If one knows the nature, order and distinctions of the levels explained above without error and cultivates calm abiding, one can easily generate faultless meditative stabilisation in about a year.

This has been a treatment of the topic of calm abiding that applies to objects in general. In particular, if one cultivates calm abiding taking the mind itself as the object, additional advantages are found. One identifies one's own mind. The mind is as vacuous as space, not having any physical qualities such as form or shape. It is something that merely perceives whatever aspects of an object appear to it with vivid clarity. Once the mind has been identified to be like this, one then engages in the nine states, the relinquishing of the five faults, the application of the eight antidotes and so forth, as has been explained above in the discussion of objects in general. One thus cultivates calm abiding.

This has been a mere enumeration of the elements of calm abiding in the sense of my having made an extreme abbreviation of Maitreya's and Asaṅga's instructions. The measure of having achieved calm abiding is that once physical and then mental pliancy have been achieved, one attains a pliancy of immovability, which is the mind's abiding one-pointedly on its object. At that time one achieves an actual calm abiding which is included in the preparation stage for the first concentration. Of the three realms, this concentration belongs to the form realm. Having attained calm abiding, the mind is serviceable, and no matter on what type of virtuous object or meaning it is set, the mind remains there one-pointedly.

Through the force of this, the ability of the mind to comprehend a meaning is very great.

Training in Higher Wisdom

How then does one progress in the training of wisdom?

In general, there are five types of wisdom, but the chief are the wisdom that cognises conventionalities, or the knowledge of nominalities, and the wisdom that cognises the ultimate, or the knowledge of the mode of being. Each of these has numerous aspects, but the wisdom to be discussed here is the one that, when generated in one's mental continuum, can completely overcome the afflicting obstructions and the obstructions to omniscience.

What is emptiness, the object of this wisdom?

Emptiness is the final mode of being of all phenomena. It does not, for instance, arise through the compassionate activities of Buddhas or through the actions of sentient beings. Each and every phenomenon, from the very fact of its coming into existence, is established as having the nature of emptiness. In a sūtra it says, 'Whether the Tathāgatas appear or not, the nature and reality of phenomena just abides.'

What is the mode of being of phenomena?

Candrakīrti's commentary on Āryadeva's *Four Hundred* says, 'Here, "self" is an inherent existence (svabhāva) of phenomena, that is, a non-dependence on another. The non-existence of this [type of self] is selflessness.' Thus, inherent existence is the object of negation, and a mere negative of inherent existence is called an emptiness.

How does one ascertain such an emptiness?

Although all phenomena have always had a nature of emptiness, we have been unable to cognise them as such. The method for cognising the meaning of emptiness is to ascertain an emptiness through relying on the Mādhyamika style of reasoning. In general, the nature or mode of being of phenomena and the way that they appear to our mind are opposite and contradictory. Though the mode of being of phenomena is that they do not inherently exist, because of beginning-less conditioning to the conception of inherent existence, whatever phenomena appear to our minds appear to exist inherently, and we conceive them as existing inherently. Because, on the basis of this, the way that phenomena appear to our minds and their actual mode of being are opposite, their mode of appearance to our minds and our mode of adhering are totally fallacious. In particular, a consciousness conceiving inherent existence is a wrong consciousness that is mistaken with respect to its referent object. Therefore, one should gain conviction that the referent object of the mind—a mind that, until now, very forcefully assented to this false appearance of inherent existence, thinking, 'This truly exists'—is non-existent. Once the referent object of the conception of inherent existence is known to be non-existent, one can easily ascertain emptiness, the mode of being of all phenomena, that is, their non-inherent existence.

With respect to this, it is initially important to ascertain how our mind misconceives [the nature of things]. To us beginners, each and every phenomenon appears to exist inherently. For instance, when one thinks to oneself, 'I, I', a self-sufficient 'I' appears, as if it were totally unrelated, different from, or independent of one's own body, mind, collection of mental and physical aggregates and continuum. If one clearly ascertains this mode of appearance and mode of adherence to the appearance, then one should analyse as follows. If this 'I' existed the way it appears, as if it were completely independent of one's own mental and physical aggregates, types, and sources, would it be one with the aggregates or different from them?

If the 'I' and the mental and physical aggregates were the

same, there would be no way to make the many divisions of the aggregates, types, sources and so forth; the aggregates would have to be one [like the 'I']. Or, just as there are aggregates, types and sources, so there would have to be many 'I's'. Furthermore, when the form aggregates of this life, for instance, are destroyed, the 'I' would also have to be destroyed. Thus, there is no way that the 'I' and the aggregates can be one.

Also, if the 'I' and aggregates were self-sufficiently different, they would be different in the sense that the one would not depend on the other. Then, when my body is sick, it would not mean that 'I' am sick, and when my stomach is full, it would not mean that 'I' am full. However, this is not the case. My body's being sick means that 'I' am sick and that suffering arises in the mind. Thus, there is no way that the 'I' and the mental and physical aggregates could be unrelatedly different.

Further, apart from sameness or difference, there is no other mode of subsistence of the 'I' and the aggregates. For, once there is an 'I' which, in accordance with its appearance, exists as if it were inherently existent, it must be either one with the aggregates or different from the aggregates. There is not at all any way of subsistence other than as one of these two.

Based on this, because the 'I' that so agreeably appears to our minds to be inherently existent is not the same as one's own aggregates and is not different from them, such an 'I' does not exist at all. Through ascertaining its non-existence thus, it is understood that on the one hand such an 'I' as presently appears to our minds does not exist, but on the other hand the 'I' is not totally non-existent. Conventionally, a merely imputedly existent 'I', a nominality, remains. This imputedly existent 'I' which is a mere nominality, can achieve resources, such as food and drink, and can own and use things, such as clothing. This 'I', which is the wanderer in cyclic existence, the practitioner of religion and the attainer of liberation, can be presented easily, without the least difficulty.

It is, therefore, free of the four extremes, which are: inherent existence, total non-existence, both of these, and neither of them. Nāgārjuna says in his *Fundamental Text Called 'Wisdom'* (XV. 10):

'Existence' is a holding to permanence,
'Non-existence' is a view of nihilism.

And:

Not existent, not non-existent, not both
And not something that is not both.

When the 'I' is ascertained as being free of the four extremes and as only imputedly existent, that is, a mere nominality, then one has ascertained a subtle selflessness relative to the 'I' as a base of selflessness. One should then switch the reasoning to other things and apply it to one's eyes and so forth, to external phenomena such as forms, sounds, tastes and odours, and even to emptiness itself. Through reasoning, it can be proved that all phenomena do not exist independently.

With respect to the meaning of all phenomena not being inherently existent, one should first hear about emptiness from reading the great books in depth; and then, in dependence on hearing about it from others, one generates the wisdom that arises from hearing. Then, in dependence on thinking again and again about its meaning, one generates the wisdom that arises from thinking. When one has gained lengthy familiarity with one-pointed meditation on the meaning that has been deeply ascertained, the wisdom that arises from meditation is attained. This occurs when the capacity of one's mind is extremely powerful through having formerly achieved calm abiding and one abides one-pointedly on the meaning of emptiness. A bliss of physical and mental pliancy is generated at this time, just as it was on the occasion of calm abiding. The difference is that the bliss of mental and physical pliancy on the occasion of calm abiding is induced by the force of stabilising meditation, but now a bliss of mental and physical pliancy that is induced by the power of analysis is generated. When this special meditative stabilisation, conjoined with such bliss, is achieved, one attains special insight. Since this special insight arises within the context of emptiness being the object, it is a meditative stabilisation that is a union of calm abiding and special insight apprehending emptiness.

At that point one has generated the sign of the path of preparation which was explained above. Further, when one cognises emptiness directly for the first time, the path of seeing is attained, and step by step the intellectually acquired and innate obstructions are removed. Finally, one is able to overcome completely and forever the afflicting obstructions and the obstructions to omniscience as well as their latent predispositions.

This has been an extremely brief account of how to practise the training of wisdom. In terms of superiority and inferiority, the succeeding trainings are superior to those that precede them. However, in terms of the order of their generation in one's continuum, the former trainings are like a basis or support for generating the latter, and therefore the training in ethics is most important in the beginning.

If one proceeds in the paths of the three trainings, taking as a basis the proper practice of refuge as well as understanding actions and their effects, the rank of liberation can be obtained. If, in addition to these, the precious mind of enlightenment (bodhicitta), which is induced by love and mercy, is cultivated and if one then practises the three trainings in conjunction with an aspiration for highest enlightenment for the sake of all sentient beings, the rank of omniscience, the superior liberation, can be obtained.

The Mind of Enlightenment

How is the mind of enlightenment cultivated?

One must consider not one's own welfare alone but the welfare of all sentient beings. Like oneself, all sentient beings are afflicted by suffering; thus, even the smallest insect is similar to oneself in not wanting suffering and wanting happiness. Although sentient beings do not want suffering, they do not know how to forsake it, and although they want happiness, they do not know how to achieve it. Since they are unable to do this by themselves, one must become able oneself to free sentient beings from suffering as well as from its causes and establish them in a state of happiness.

There is no way to forsake suffering and achieve happiness other than for the causes, which exist in the continuums of sentient beings and which give rise to suffering, to be removed and for the causes of happiness to be achieved in their own continuums. The Blessed One said:

> Buddhas neither wash sins away with water,
> Nor remove beings' sufferings with their hands,
> Nor transfer their realisations to others; beings
> Are freed through the teachings of the truth, the nature of
> things.

There is no way to remove sins in the way that grime is washed away with water or to remove suffering like picking out a thorn. There is no way for a Buddha to transfer the realisations in his own continuum and give them to others. Then, how is suffering removed? Sentient beings are liberated from all suffering in dependence on the teachings of reality, the mode of being of phenomena.

Thus, sentient beings are freed through teaching them what is to be adopted and what is to be discarded. In order to teach sentient beings what is to be adopted and what is to be discarded, one must first know and understand these oneself. Also, there is no one other than a Buddha who is able to teach paths without error in accordance with the various dispositions, thoughts and interests, not just of a few sentient beings but of all. Since this is so, one is certain to attain the rank of Buddhahood as a conducive circumstance for achieving one's aim, the welfare of sentient beings. For example, if a man is stricken with thirst, his thirst is mainly removed by drinking water and so forth. Yet, he must first seek a vessel in which to drink the water. Similarly, here also, although one's main purpose is to liberate sentient beings from suffering as well as its causes, in order to do this one must first develop an aspiration to achieve the rank of highest enlightenment from seeing the necessity for doing so.

If such an attitude is generated, it is called a mind of enlightenment, an aspiration to highest enlightenment for the sake of all sentient beings. If in conjunction with such an attitude one engages in virtues, great or small, such as meditating on emptiness, cultivating calm abiding, taking refuge, forsaking killing, these virtuous deeds—when they are conjoined with this altruistic attitude—naturally become causes of omniscience.

II
The Key to
the Middle Way

A Treatise on the Realisation
of Emptiness

TENZIN GYATSO
The Fourteenth Dalai Lama

Translated by Jeffrey Hopkins and
Lati Rimpoche
with Alexander Berzin, Jonathan Landaw
and Anne Klein

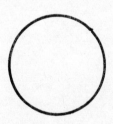

Translators' Note

The text was translated by Jeffrey Hopkins, who orally re-translated the English into Tibetan for verification and correction by Lati Rimpoche and then worked with Alexander Berzin, Jonathan Landaw, and Anne Klein to improve the presentation in English.

The Key to the Middle Way

Homage to the perfection of wisdom.

> I respectfully bow down to the Conqueror,
> Protector of all beings through boundless compassion,
> With dominion over glorious wisdom and deeds, but who
> Like an illusion is only designated by words and thoughts.

> I will explain here in brief terms the essence
> Of the ambrosia of his good speech,
> The mode of the union of emptiness and dependent-arising,
> To increase the insight of those with burgeoning intellect.

We all want happiness and do not want suffering. Moreover, achieving happiness and eliminating suffering depend upon the deeds of body, speech and mind. As the deeds of body and speech depend upon the mind, we must therefore constructively transform the mind. The ways of constructively transforming the mind are to cause mistaken states of consciousness not to be generated and good states of consciousness to be both generated and increased.

What are the determinants, in this context, of a bad state of consciousness? A state of consciousness, once produced, may initially cause ourselves to become unhappy and our previously calm mind suddenly to become excited or tense. This may then act as the cause of hard breathing, nervous sweating, illness, and so forth. From these, in turn, bad deeds of body and speech may arise, which directly or indirectly may also cause hardship for others. All states of consciousness that give rise to such a causal sequence are assigned as bad. The determinants of good states of consciousness, on the other hand, are just the opposite. All states of consciousness that cause the bestowal of the fruit of happiness and peace upon ourselves or others, either superficially or in depth, are assigned as good.

As for ways of causing mistaken states of consciousness not to be generated, there are such means as undergoing brain operations, ingesting various types of drugs, making our awareness dull as if overcome with drowsiness, and making ourselves senseless as if in deep sleep. However, apart from only occasional superficial help, these mostly do more harm than good from the point of view of deep solutions.

Therefore, the way of beneficially transforming the mind is as follows. First we must think about the disadvantages of bad states of consciousness, identifying them from our own personal experience. Then we must recognise the good states of consciousness. If familiarity with them is developed through thinking again and again about their advantages and about their supporting validators, then the various types of good states of consciousness will become stronger. This occurs through the force of familiarity and through these good states of consciousness having valid foundations and being qualities dependent on the mind [and thus capable of limitless development]. Then, it is natural that the defective states of consciousness will decrease in strength. Thereby, in time, sure signs of goodness will appear in the mind.

Many such different methods of transforming the mind have been taught by the many great teachers of this world, in accordance with individual times and places and in accordance with the minds of individual trainees. Among these, many methods of taming the mind have been taught in the books of the Buddhists. From among these, a little will be said here about the view of emptiness.

Views of selflessness are taught in both Buddhist vehicles, the Mahāyāna and the Hīnayāna, and with respect to the Mahāyāna in both sūtra and tantra divisions. When a Buddhist and a non-Buddhist are differentiated by way of behaviour, the difference is whether or not the person takes refuge in the

Three Jewels. When they are differentiated by way of view, the difference is whether or not the person asserts the views which are the four seals testifying to a doctrine's being the word of the Buddha. The four seals are:

All products are impermanent.
All contaminated things are miserable.
All phenomena are empty and selfless.
Nirvāṇa is peace.

Therefore, all Buddhists assert that all phenomena are empty and selfless.

With respect to the meaning of selflessness, there is a selflessness of persons, that is the non-existence of persons as substantial entities or self-sufficient entities. This is asserted by all four Buddhist schools of tenets: Vaibhāṣika, Sautrāntika, Cittamātra and Mādhyamika. The Cittamātrins assert, in addition, a selflessness of phenomena that is an emptiness of objects and subjects as different entities. The Mādhyamikas assert a selflessness of phenomena that is an emptiness of inherent existence.

The meaning of the views of the lower and higher schools of tenets differs greatly in coarseness and subtlety. However, if understanding is developed with respect to the lower systems, this serves as a means of deep ascertainment of the higher views; therefore, it is very helpful to do so. Here, selflessness is to be discussed in accordance with the Mādhyamika system, and within the division of the Mādhyamika into Svātantrika and Prāsaṅgika, in accordance with the Prāsaṅgika system.

Question: Did the Blessed One set forth all these different schools of tenets? If he did, on what sūtras do each rely? Also, does the difference of status and depth of the schools of tenets necessarily depend on scriptural authority?

Answer: The different views of the four schools of tenets were set forth by the Blessed One himself in accordance with the mental capacities of his trainees, whether superior, middling, or low. Some trainees were likely to fall into views of nihilism or were in danger of losing faith if taught selflessness. For them Buddha even taught the existence of a self in some sūtras. Also, some trainees were likely to go either to the extreme of eternity or to the extreme of annihilation if Buddha answered their questions in the positive or the negative. For them Buddha did not say either 'exists' or 'does not exist', but remained silent, as in the case of the fourteen inexpressible views. Also, with respect to the modes of selflessness, Buddha set forth many forms as was briefly explained above.

The sūtras on which each of the schools relies are as follows. The Vaibhāṣika and Sautrāntika schools of tenets rely mainly on the sūtras of the first wheel of doctrine, such as the *Sūtra on the Four Truths* (*Catuḥsatya*). The Cittamātra school of tenets relies mainly on the sūtras of the last wheel of doctrine, such as the *Unravelling of the Thought Sūtra* (*Saṃdhinirmocana*). The Mādhyamika school relies mainly on the sūtras of the middle wheel of doctrine, such as the *Hundred Thousand Stanza Perfection of Wisdom Sūtra* (*Śatasāhasrikāprajñāpāramitā*). There are ways of presenting the three series of wheels of doctrine from the point of view of place, time, subject and trainee [but this is not a place for such a lengthy discussion].

If it were necessary to differentiate the status and depth of the schools' different views in dependence on scriptural authority, then, since the individual sūtras each say that the system which it teaches is the superior system, we may wonder which scripture should be held as true. If one scripture were held to be true, we would then wonder how the other discordant sūtras should be considered. But, if the modes of truth of one sūtra and the non-truth of the others were necessarily provable only by scriptural authority, then the process would be endless. Therefore, the differentiation of the superiority and inferiority of views must rely only on reasoning.

Thus, the Mahāyāna sūtras say that it is necessary to

distinguish what requires interpretation and what is definitive. Thinking of this, Buddha says in a sūtra:

> Monks and scholars should
> Well analyse my words,
> Like gold [to be tested through] melting, cutting and polishing,
> And then adopt them, but not for the sake of showing me respect.

In his *Ornament of the Mahāyāna Sūtras* (*Mahāyānasūtrālaṃkāra*), Maitreya commented well on the meaning of Buddha's thought in that statement and set forth the four reliances:

1 One should not rely on the person of a teacher, but on the tenets or doctrines that he teaches.
2 One should not rely merely on the euphony and so forth of his words, but on their meaning.
3 With respect to the meaning, one should not rely on those teachings that require interpretation. Such interpretation would be necessary if there were some other non-explicit base in the teacher's thought, if there were a purpose for the teaching's being stated in interpretable form, and if the explicit words of the teaching were susceptible to refutation. One should rely, rather, on those teachings that have definitive meaning, that is, which do not require interpretation.
4 With respect to the definitive meaning, one should not rely on a dualistic consciousness, but on a non-conceptual wisdom.

With respect to a non-conceptual wisdom that apprehends a profound emptiness, one first cultivates a conceptual consciousness that apprehends an emptiness, and when a clear perception of the object of meditation arises, this becomes a non-conceptual wisdom. Moreover, the initial generation of that conceptual consciousness must depend solely on a correct reasoning. Fundamentally, therefore, this process traces back solely to a reasoning, which itself must fundamentally trace back to valid experiences common to ourselves and others. Thus, it is the thought of Dignāga and Dharmakīrti, the kings of reasoning, that fundamentally a reasoning derives from an obvious experience.

Question: For the sake of improving the mind what is the use of developing valid cognisers and states of consciousness that realise the presentations of views of emptiness? What practitioners need is a sense of practical application and goodness; it is the scholars who need to be learned.

Answer: There are many stages in the improvement of the mind. There are some in which analysis of reasons is not necessary, such as when trusting faith alone is to be cultivated single-pointedly. Not much strength, however, is achieved by just that alone. Especially for developing the mind into limitless goodness, it is not sufficient merely to familiarise the mind with its object of meditation. The object of meditation must involve reasoning. Further, it is not sufficient for the object to have reasons in general; the meditator himself must know them and have found a conviction in them. Therefore, it is impossible for the superior type of practitioner not to have intelligence.

Still, if we were forced to choose between a sense of practical application and learnedness, a sense of practical application would be more important, for one who has this will receive the full benefit of whatever he knows. The mere learnedness of one whose mind is not tamed can produce and increase bad states of consciousness, which cause unpleasantness for himself and others instead of the happiness and peace of mind that were intended. One could become jealous of those higher than oneself, competitive with equals and proud and contemptuous towards those lower and so forth. It is as if medicine had become poison. Because such danger is great, it is very important to have a composite of learnedness, a sense of practical application and goodness, without having learnedness destroy the sense of practical application or having the sense of practical application destroy learnedness.

Concerning the improvement of the mind, in order to ascertain the meaning of a selflessness or of an emptiness, it is necessary to ascertain first the meaning of just what a phenomenon is empty of when we refer to 'an emptiness'. The Bodhisattva Śāntideva says in his *Engaging in the Bodhisattva Deeds* (*Bodhicaryāvatāra*, IX.140):

> Without identifying the imputed thing
> Its non-existence cannot be apprehended.

Just so, without ascertaining that of which a phenomenon is empty, an understanding of its emptiness does not develop.

Question: Of what is it that a phenomenon is empty?

Answer: [When we Prāsaṅgikas speak of an emptiness, we are not referring to the situation in which one object is empty of some other existent entity. Thus] though we may commonly speak of an 'empty rainbow', since the rainbow is empty of anything tangible, this type of an emptiness is not what we have in mind. [This is because anything tangible can exist separate from an empty rainbow; and, moreover, there is still something positive about this rainbow empty of anything tangible, such as its having colour.] Though we may also speak of 'empty space', since space is empty of anything physical, this too is not an example of what we mean by an emptiness [although here there is nothing else positive implied about space, which is the mere absence of anything physical. This is because here too anything physical can exist separate from empty space.] Rather, when we speak of a phenomenon as being empty, we are referring to its being empty of its own inherent existence [which does not exist at all, let alone exist separate from the phenomenon. In one respect, then, there is a similarity here in that just as a rainbow is naturally empty of anything tangible—it never has been tangible—so too, a phenomenon is naturally empty of its own inherent existence— it never has had inherent existence.] Further, it is not that the object of the negation [inherent existence] formerly existed and is later eliminated, like the forest which existed yesterday and which is burned by fire today, with the result that the area is now empty of the forest. Rather, this is an emptiness of an object of negation [inherent existence], which from beginning- less time has never been known validly to exist.

Also, with respect to the way in which a phenomenon is empty of the object of negation, it is not like a table top being empty of flowers. [There, the object of the negation, flowers, is an entity separate from the base of the negation, the table top. With the object of the negation being inherent existence, however, we are not negating an entity separate from the base of the negation, a phenomenon, but rather we are negating a mode of existence of the base of the negation itself. Thus] we mean that the base of the negation, a phenomenon, does not exist in the manner of the object of the negation, its own inherent existence. Therefore, without ascertaining just what the object of the negation is of which phenomena are empty, that is, without ascertaining the measure of what self is in the theory of selflessness, we cannot understand the meaning of an emptiness. A mere vacuity without any sense of 'The object of the negation is this' and 'It is not that' is utterly not the meaning of an emptiness.

Question: What is the use of going to all the trouble of first understanding what something definitely non-existent [inherent existence] would mean if it were existent; and then, after that, viewing it as definitely non-existent?

Answer: It is common worldly knowledge that by believing untrue information to be true we fall into confusion and are harmed. Similarly, by believing phenomena to be inherently existent when in fact they are not inherently existent, we are also harmed. For example, with respect to the different ways in which there can be a consciousness of 'I', there is a definite difference between the way the 'I' is apprehended when desire, hatred, pride and so forth are generated based on this 'I', and the way the 'I' is apprehended when we are relaxed without any of those attitudes being manifest. Similarly, there is the mere consciousness that apprehends an article in a store before we buy it, and there is the consciousness apprehending that article after it has been bought, when it is adhered to as 'mine' and grasped with attachment. Both these consciousnesses have the same object, and in both cases the mode of appearance of the article is the appearance of it as inherently existent. However, there is the difference of the presence or absence of our adhering to it as inherently or independently existent.

Also, when we see ten men, just from merely seeing them it appears to us that ten men exist there objectively or inherently; however, there is no certainty that we will go on to adhere at that time to this appearance of ten objectively or inherently existent men and posit truth to it. [If we were to posit truth to the appearance of these men as being inherently existent, the process of doing so would be as follows.] For either right or wrong reasons, a strong thought [based on having conceived these ten men to be inherently existent] will be generated, which incorrectly considers one from among these ten men as good or bad. At that time, our intellect will falsely superimpose on the appearance of this man a goodness or badness that exceeds what actually exists. Desire and hatred will then be generated, and consequently we will adhere at that time to this object [the appearance of an inherently existent good or bad man] tightly from the depths of our mind as true, most true.

Therefore, a consciousness conceiving inherent existence precedes any bad consciousness, leading it on by the nose, and also accompanies, or aids, many other bad consciousnesses as well. Thus, if there were no ignorance conceiving inherent existence, then there would be no chance for desire, hatred and so forth to be generated. Since that is so, it is important to identify the beginningless emptiness of the object of the negation, which is to say, it is important to identify as non-existent that non-existent entity [inherent existence] which has never validly been known to exist. Once we have made this identification, it is necessary to generate conviction in it as well. The purpose of this process is to cease the arising of incorrect thoughts, inexhaustible like ripples on an ocean, which arise through the force of the appearance of inherent existence as existent, even though it is non-existent, and through the force of the adherence to that false appearance as true. As Nāgārjuna says in the eighteenth chapter of his *Fundamental Text Called 'Wisdom'* (*Prajñā-nāma-mūlamadhyamakakārikā*, XVIII. 4–5):

> When the thought of the internal
> And the external as 'I' and 'mine'
> Has perished, grasping ceases
> And through that cessation birth ceases.

> When actions and afflictions cease, there is liberation;
> They arise from false conceptions, these arise
> From the elaborations [of false views on inherent
> Existence]; elaborations cease in emptiness.

Inherent existence has never been validly known to exist; therefore, it is impossible for there to be any phenomenon that exists through its own power. Since it is experienced that mere dependent-arisings, which are in fact empty of inherent existence, do cause all forms of help and harm, these are established as existent. Thus, mere dependent-arisings do exist. Therefore, all phenomena exist in the manner of appearing as varieties of dependent-arisings. They appear this way without passing beyond the sphere or condition of having just this nature of being utterly non-inherently existent. Therefore, all phenomena have two entities: one entity that is its superficial mode of appearance and one entity that is its deep mode of being. These two are called respectively conventional truths and ultimate truths.

The Superior (Ārya) Nāgārjuna says in his *Fundamental Text Called 'Wisdom'* (XXIV. 8):

> Doctrines taught by the Buddhas
> Rely wholly on the two truths,
> Conventional and worldly truths
> And truths that are ultimate.

Also, the glorious Candrakīrti says in his *Supplement to (Nāgārjuna's) 'Treatise on the Middle Way'* (*Madhyamakāvatāra*, VI. 23)[1]:

> [Buddha] said that all phenomena have two entities,
> Those found by perceivers of the true and of the false;
> Objects of perceivers of the true are realities,
> Objects of perceivers of the false are conventional truths.

The divisions of ultimate truths will be briefly explained below. Conventional truths themselves are divided into the real and the unreal just from the point of view of an ordinary worldly consciousness. Candrakīrti says (*Supplement*, VI. 24–25):

> Also those which perceive falsities are said to be of two types,
> Those with clear senses and those having defective ones.
> A consciousness having a defective sense is said to be
> Wrong in relation to one with a sense that is sound.
>
> Objects realised by the world and apprehended
> By the six non-defective senses are only true
> From a worldly point of view, the rest are presented
> As unreal only from the viewpoint of the world.

The purpose of knowing thus the presentation of the two truths is as follows. Since it is utterly necessary to be involved with these appearances which bring about varieties of good and bad effects, it is necessary to know the two natures, superficial and deep, of these objects to which we are related. For example, there may be a cunning and deceptive neighbour with whom it is always necessary for us to interact and to whom we have related by way of an estimation of him that accords only with his [pleasant] external appearance. The various losses that we have sustained in this relationship are not due to the fault of our merely having interacted with that man. Rather, the fault lies with our mistaken manner of relating to him. Further, because of not knowing the man's nature, we have not estimated him properly and have thereby been deceived. Therefore, if that man's external appearance and his fundamental nature had both been well known, we would have related to him with a reserve appropriate to his nature and with whatever corresponded to his capacities, and so forth. Had we done this, we would not have sustained any losses.

Similarly, if phenomena had no deep mode of being other than their external or superficial mode of being, and if thus the way they appeared and the way they existed were in agreement, then it would be sufficient to hold that conventional modes of appearance are true just as they appear, and to place confidence in them. However, this is not so. Though phenomena appear as if true, most true, ultimately they are not true. Therefore, phenomena abide in the middle way, not truly or inherently existent and also not utterly non-existent. This view, or way of viewing—the knowledge of such a mode of being, just as it is— is called the view of the middle way.

With respect to this, the way in which there is no inherent existence or self is as follows. Whatever objects appear to us now—forms, sounds and so forth which are cognised by the eyes, ears and so on, or objects cognised by the mind, or objects of experience and so forth—these objects are the bases of negation, in relation to which the object of that negation, inherent existence, is negated. They appear to be inherently existent, or existing as independent entities, or existing objectively. Therefore, all consciousnesses are mistaken except for the wisdom that directly cognises emptiness.

Question: [If all those consciousnesses that are not directly cognising emptiness are mistaken, does this mean that] there are no valid cognisers which could certify the existence of conventionally existent phenomena, such as forms and so on? Or, does this mean that since the criterion for a phenomenon's existing conventionally would have to be its existing for a mistaken, perverse consciousness [rather than its existing for a valid cogniser], it would follow that the non-existence of any phenomenon could not occur [because any phenomenon could be cognised by a mistaken consciousness]?

Answer: It is not contradictory for a consciousness to be mistaken, on the one hand, because objects appear to it as if they inherently existed, and, on the other, for it to be valid, because it is not deceived with respect to its main object. For example, a visual consciousness perceiving a form is indeed a mistaken consciousness because the form appears to it as inherently existent. However, to the extent that it perceives the form as a form and does not *conceive* the form to be inherently existent, it is a valid cogniser. Not only that, but a visual consciousness perceiving a form is also a valid cogniser with respect to the appearance of the form and even with respect to the appearance of the form's seeming to be inherently existent. All dualistic consciousnesses, therefore, are valid direct cognisers with respect to their own objects of perception, because in the expression, 'a consciousness knowing its object', a consciousness refers to a clear knower which is generated in the image of its object through the force of the appearance of its object.

Further, the criterion for a phenomenon's existing conventionally is not merely its existing for a mistaken, perverse consciousness. For example, an appearance of falling hairs manifestly appears to the visual consciousness of someone with cataract. Because his consciousness has been generated in the image of falling hairs, it is a valid, direct cogniser with respect to that object of perception. However, since the falling hairs, which are the basis of such an appearance, are utterly non-existent, the consciousness is deceived with respect to its main object. Thus, because this consciousness of falling hairs is directly contradicted by a consciousness with a valid mode of perception, it is asserted to be a wrong consciousness. How could existing for this mistaken consciousness be the criterion for a phenomenon's existing conventionally?

In short, it is said that though there is no phenomenon that is not posited by the mind, whatever the mind posits is not necessarily existent.

When a phenomenon appears thus to be inherently existent, if the phenomenon existed in the same way as it appeared, then the entity of its inherent existence would necessarily become clearer when its mode of existence was carefully analysed. For example, even in terms of what is widely known in the world, if something is true, it becomes clearer and its foundation more firm the more one analyses it. Therefore, when sought, it must definitely be findable. If, on the contrary, it is false, then when it is analysed and sought, it becomes unclear, and in the end it cannot stand up. Nāgārjuna's *Precious Garland* (*Ratnā-valī*, 52–53) says:

A form seen from a distance
Is seen clearly by those nearby.
If a mirage were water, why
Is water not seen by those nearby?

The way this world is seen
As real by those afar
Is not so seen by those nearby,
[For whom it is] signless like a mirage.

Let us give an example. When it is said and thought that human beings should have happiness, a human who is one who should have happiness appears boldly to our mind as if existing in his own right. To create human happiness, one must achieve the favourable circumstances for physical pleasures such as food, clothing, shelter, medicines and transportation for the body, and the favourable circumstances for mental pleasures such as higher education, respectability, good disposition and tranquility for the mind. It is necessary to create a human's happiness through physical and mental pleasures. That being so, if we search, wondering what the real human is, we find that his body and mind individually are not the human, and there is also no identifying, 'This is the human,' separately from these two.

Similarly, when we have met an acquaintance named 'Lucky', we say, for instance, 'I saw Lucky,' 'Lucky has become old,' or 'Lucky has become fat.' Without analysing or examining those statements, seeing Lucky's body is said to be seeing Lucky; seeing his body weaker is said to be seeing Lucky weaker; and seeing his body larger is said to be seeing Lucky larger. A consciousness that perceives such without analysis is not a wrong consciousness, and these statements also are not false. [However] when analysis is done, a real Lucky himself who is the possessor of the body is not to be seen, and his ageing and becoming fat also cannot stand up to analysis. Further, with respect to the goodness or badness of Lucky's mind, Lucky is designated as a good man or a bad man. But Lucky's mind itself is not Lucky. In short, there is not the slightest part which is Lucky among the mere collection of Lucky's mind and body, his continuum, or individual parts. Therefore, dependent on the mere collection of Lucky's body and mind, we designate 'Lucky'. As Nāgārjuna says in his *Precious Garland* (80):

> The person is not earth, not water,
> Not fire, not wind, not space,
> Not consciousness and not all of them;
> What person is there other than these?

E

Further, with respect to the statement, 'I saw Lucky's body,' seeing merely the external skin from among the many parts of the body, flesh, skin, bones and so forth, functions as seeing his body. Even if the blood, bones and so forth are not seen, it does not mean that the body is not seen. To see a body it is not necessary to see all of the body; seeing even a small part can function as seeing the body. However, sometimes by the force of general custom, if a certain amount is not seen, it cannot function as a seeing of the body. As above, if the body is divided into its individual parts, legs, arms and so on, a body is not found. Also, the legs and arms can be divided into toes and fingers, the toes and fingers into joints and the joints into upper and lower portions; these can be divided into small parts and even the smallest parts into parts corresponding with the directions. When they are divided in this way, none of these entities are findable. Also, if the smallest particle were directionally partless, that is, if it had no sides, then no matter how many directionally partless particles were collected, they could never be arranged side by side to form a mass.

Furthermore, Lucky is said to be happy or unhappy according to whether his mind is at ease or not. What is this mind which is the basis of this determination? It does not exist as anything physical, it lacks anything tangible, any object can appear to it, and it exists as an entity of mere knowing. Further, it is like this when it is not analysed; but when it is analysed, it is unfindable. When Lucky's mind is happy, the entity of that mind is what is to be analysed. If it is divided into individual moments, there is no mass that is a composite of the many former and later moments. At the time of the later moments, the former moments have ceased; therefore, the former ones have gone and their conscious entity has disappeared. Because the future moments have not yet been produced, they are not existing now. Also, the single present moment is not separate from what has already been produced and what has not yet been produced. Therefore, when it is sought thus, one is unable to establish a present consciousness. When the happy mind, which is the object discussed in 'His mind is happy,' is sought, it is utterly unfindable. In short, happy and unhappy minds and so forth are designated to a mere collection of their own former and future moments. Even the shortest moment is imputed to its own parts; it has the individual parts of a beginning and an end. If a moment were partless, there could be no continuum composed of them.

Similarly, when an external object such as a table appears to the mind, a naturally existent or independent table appears. Let us analyse this table by dividing it into a whole and parts. In general, the table is put as the base of its qualities, and by examining its qualities such as shape, colour, material and size, we can speak of its value, quality and so forth. For example, when we say 'This table is good, but its colour is not good,' there is a table that is the base of the estimation of the quality of its colour. A base of qualities that possesses these qualities does [conventionally] exist, but the qualities and parts individually are not themselves the base of the qualities. Also, after eliminating the qualities and parts, a base of these qualities is not findable. If there is no such base, then since qualities are necessarily established in dependence on a base of qualities and, moreover, since a base of qualities is necessarily established in dependence on qualities, the qualities also will not exist.

Let us illustrate this with the example of a rosary which has one hundred and eight beads. The whole, the one rosary, has one hundred and eight beads as its parts. The parts and the whole are [conventionally] different; yet, when the parts are eliminated, a rosary cannot be found. Because the rosary is one and its parts are many, the rosary is not the same as its parts. When the parts are eliminated, there is no rosary which exists separately; therefore, it is not inherently or fundamentally different from its parts. Because the rosary does not exist separate from its parts, it does not inherently depend on its parts, nor do the parts inherently depend on it. Also, the beads do not inherently belong to the rosary. Similarly, since the shape of the rosary is one of its qualities, this shape is not the rosary. Also, the collection of the beads and the string is the basis in dependence on which the rosary is imputed; therefore, it is not the rosary. If it is sought in this way, a rosary is unfindable as any of the seven extremes. Further, if the individual beads are sought as above, that is, as one with their parts, or different from their parts and so forth, they are unfindable as well. Furthermore, since forests, armies, continents, and countries are imputed to aggregations of many parts, when each is analysed as to whether it is this or not that, it is utterly unfindable.

Further, it is extremely clear that good and bad, tall and short, big and small, enemy and friend, father and son and so forth are all imputations of the one based on the other. Also earth, water, fire, wind and so on are each imputed in dependence on their parts. Space is imputed in dependence on its parts, which pervade the directions. Also, Buddhas and sentient beings, cyclic existence and nirvāṇa and so forth are only just imputed in dependence on their parts and their bases of imputation.

Just as it is widely known that, 'An effect is produced from causes,' so production does exist [conventionally]. However, let us analyse the meaning of production. If effects were produced causelessly, they would either always be produced or would never be produced. If they were produced from themselves, it would be purposeless for what has already attained its own entity to be produced again; and if what had already been produced is produced again, then there is the consequent fallacy that its reproduction would be endless. If effects were produced from entities other than themselves, they would be produced from everything, both from what are considered conventionally to be their causes and from what are not [since both are equally other]. Or, it would be contradictory for effects to depend on causes [for, being totally separate, they could not be inter-related]. Production from both self and others is not possible either [because of the faults in both these positions demonstrated separately above]. Thus, if the meaning of the designation 'production' is sought, production is not capable of being established. As the Superior Nāgārjuna says in his *Fundamental Text Called 'Wisdom'* (I. 1):

> There is never production
> Anywhere of any phenomenon
> From itself, from others,
> From both, or without cause.

Though it is widely known [and conventionally correct] that causes do produce effects, let us analyse these effects. If the produced effect inherently existed, how could it be correct for what already exists to be produced newly? For, causes are not needed to create it anew. In general, causes conventionally do newly create that which has not been produced or which is non-existent at the time of its causes. However, if the non-produced were inherently true as non-produced, it would be no different from being utterly non-existent; therefore, how could it be fit for production by causes? As Nāgārjuna says in his *Seventy Stanzas on Emptiness* (*Śūnyatāsaptati*):

> Because it exists, the existent is not produced;
> Because it does not exist, the non-existent is not produced.

In short, once the existence of something is necessarily dependent on causes and conditions and on others, then it is contradictory for it to exist independently. For, independence and dependence on others are contradictory. The *Questions of the King of Nāgas, Anavatapta, Sūtra* (*Anavataptanāgarāja-paripṛcchā*) says:

> That which is produced from causes is not [inherently] produced,
> It does not have an inherent nature of production.
> That which depends on causes is said to be
> Empty; he who knows emptiness is aware.

Nāgārjuna's *Fundamental Text Called 'Wisdom'* (XXIV. 19) says:

> Because there are no phenomena
> Which are not dependent-arisings,
> There are no phenomena
> Which are not empty.

Āryadeva says in his *Four Hundred* (*Catuḥśataka*, XIV. 23):

> That which has dependent-arising
> Cannot be self-powered; since all these
> Lack independence there can be
> No self [no inherent existence].

If phenomena were not empty of a fundamental basis or of inherent existence, it would be utterly impossible for the varieties of phenomena to be transformed in dependence on causes. If they existed by way of their own fundamental basis, then no matter what type of entity they were, good, bad and so on, how could they be changed? If a good fruit tree, for instance, were inherently existent by way of its own entity or its own inner basis, how would it be true that it could become bare and ugly? If the present mode of appearance of these things to our minds were their own inner mode of being, how could we be deceived? Even in the ordinary world many discrepancies are well known between what appears and what actually is. Therefore, although beginninglessly everything has appeared as if it were inherently existent to the mind that is contaminated with the errors of ignorance, if those objects were indeed inherently existent, their inner basis would be just as they appear. In that case, when the consciousness searching for the inner basis of a phenomenon performed analysis, that inner basis would definitely become clearer. Where does the fault lie, that when sought, phenomena are not found and seemingly disappear?

Further, if things inherently existed, it would be as Candra-kīrti says in his *Supplement* (VI. 34-36)[2]:

> If the inherent existence [of phenomena] depended [on causes, the yogī
> Realising emptiness], by denying that, would be destroying phenomena;
> Therefore, [seeing] emptiness would be a cause which destroys phenomena, but since
> This is not reasonable, phenomena do not [inherently exist].
>
> When these phenomena are analysed, they are not found
> To abide as other than phenomena with the nature
> Of reality [having no inherently existent production or cessation];
> Therefore, worldly conventional truths are not to be analysed.
>
> When reality [is analysed] production
> From self and other is not admissible,
> Through the same reasoning [inherently existent production] also is not admissible
> Conventionally; how then could your [inherently existent] production be [established]?

Thus, Candrakīrti is saying that if phenomena existed naturally or inherently, it would follow that a Superior's meditative equipoise realising emptiness would cause the destruction of these phenomena. Also, it would follow that conventional truths would be able to stand up to a reasoned analysis. Further, it would follow that production would not be ultimately refuted, and that many sūtras which teach that phenomena are empty of themselves in the sense that they are empty of their own natural inherent existence would be wrong. For instance, a Mother Sūtra, the *Twenty-Five Thousand Stanza Perfection of Wisdom Sūtra* (*Pañcaviṃśatisāhasrikāprajñāpāramitā*) says, 'With respect to this, Śāriputra, when a Bodhisattva, a great being, practises the perfection of wisdom, he does not see a Bodhisattva as real. . . . Why? Śāriputra, it is like this: a Bodhisattva is empty of being an inherently existent Bodhisattva. A Bodhisattva's name also is empty of being a Bodhisattva's name. Why? That is their nature. It is like this: it is not that a form is empty on account of emptiness; emptiness is not separate from a form. A form itself is [that which is] empty; just [that which is] empty is also the form.' Further, the *Kāśyapa Chapter* in the *Pile of Jewels Sūtra* (*Ratnakūṭa*) says, 'Phenomena are not made empty by emptiness, the phenomena themselves are empty.' Therefore, all phenomena lack inherent existence or their own basic foundation.

Question: If a real man and a dream man, a form and a reflection, a real thing and a picture are the same in that they are not found when sought, would it not follow that there would be no differences among them? There would be no differences as to their truth, falsity and so forth. Thus, what would be the use of searching into the view of emptiness? For, the searcher and the view itself would be none other than non-existent.

Answer: This touches on a difficult point. There is a great danger that because of this subtle point those of immature intelligence might fall to a view of nihilism. Therefore, to avoid that, some who were skilled in means, the Svātantrika-Mādhyamika Bhāvaviveka and his spiritual sons [Jñānagarbha, Śāntarakṣita, Kamalaśīla, etc.], used reasoning to refute that phenomena exist from the point of view of their own particular mode of subsistence and without being established through their appearance to a faultless consciousness. However, they asserted natural or inherent existence conventionally. For those whose minds could not cope even with this type of truthlessness, the Cittamātrin teachers, Vasubandhu and so forth, used reasoning to refute external objects, yet asserted that the mind does truly exist. For those who could not be vessels of a teaching of the selflessness of phenomena, the proponents of truly existing external objects—the Vaibhāṣikas and Sautrāntikas—asserted in the place of emptiness a mere selflessness, which is the person's non-existence as a substantial or self-sufficient entity. The non-Buddhists could not even assert the mere selflessness of persons, and from that, therefore, they derive the necessity of asserting a permanent, partless, independent person.

Question: If it is asserted that phenomena do not exist by reason of their not being found when the object imputed is sought, that contradicts what is widely known in the world; for it goes against obvious experience. Our own experience affirms the existence of these phenomena which are all included in the terms 'environments' and 'beings'. Our own experience affirms as well the fact that varieties of help, harm, pleasure and pain are produced. Thus, what is the meaning of not being able to find such things as self and other, environments and beings, when we seek these varieties of definitely existent phenomena?

Answer: The *Twenty-Five Thousand Stanza Perfection of Wisdom Sūtra* says, 'It is thus: this "Bodhisattva" is only a name; this "perfection of wisdom" is only a name; these "forms", "feelings", "discriminations", "compositional factors", and "consciousnesses" are only names. It is thus: forms are like illusions. Feelings, discriminations, compositional factors and consciousnesses are like illusions. Illusions also are only names; they do not abide in places; they do not abide in the directions. . . . Why? It is thus: names are fabricated and imputed to the individual phenomena, names are adventitiously designated. They are all designations. When a Bodhisattva, a great being, practices the perfection of wisdom, he does not view names as real. Because he does not view them as real, he does not adhere to them. Further, O Śāriputra, when a Bodhisattva, a great being, practises the perfection of wisdom, he thinks thus: this "Bodhisattva" is only a name; this "enlightenment" is only a name; this "perfection of wisdom" is

73

only a name; these "forms" are only names; these "feelings", "discriminations", "compositional factors" and "consciousnesses" are only names. Śāriputra, it is thus: "I" for example is designated, but the "I" is unapprehendable.' In many sūtras and treatises phenomena are all said to be only names. When imputed objects are sought, they are utterly not there in any objective way. This is a sign that all phenomena are not objectively existent and are only established as existing through subjective designations and thoughts. Existing merely in this way functions as existing.

Let us explain this further in fine detail. For something to exist conventionally, it must satisfy three criteria:

1   The object must be generally well known to a conventional consciousness. Yet, if merely being well known were sufficient [to establish the conventional existence of an object], then even the commonly cited 'son of a barren woman' would exist. Therefore, for any object to exist conventionally,

2   It must not be possible for a conventional valid cogniser to contradict it. Yet, since a conventional valid cogniser cannot refute inherent existence [which otherwise would exist conventionally by merely the above two criteria],

3   It must not be possible for a reasoning that analyses the ultimate to refute it either.

Therefore, an entity existing objectively without existing merely through the force of subjective designations is the measure or meaning of what is negated; it is that of which phenomena are empty in the expression 'emptiness'. It is also called 'self' or 'object negated by reasoning'. Since it is utterly not known validly to exist, a consciousness that adheres to it as existent is called an ignorant consciousness. In general, there are many types of mere ignorance; however, that which is being explained here is the ignorance that is the root of cyclic existence, the opposite of the wisdom that cognises selflessness. Nāgārjuna's *Seventy Stanzas on Emptiness* says:

> The thought that phenomena produced
> From causes and conditions are real
> Was called ignorance by the Teacher;
> From it the twelve branches[3] arise.

A mere non-existence of the self which is the object of negation, that is, the mere non-existence of an inherent existence as apprehended by such an ignorant consciousness, is called a selflessness, a truthlessness and an emptiness. Just this is the deep mode of subsistence or final mode of being of all phenomena; therefore, it is called an ultimate truth. A consciousness that cognises it is called a consciousness cognising an emptiness.

Question: Since emptinesses are ultimate truths, do emptinesses themselves exist?

Answer: An emptiness is the way of being, or mode of existence, of the phenomenon qualified by it. Therefore, if the phenomenon qualified by an emptiness does not exist, there is no emptiness of it. The empty nature of a phenomenon is established in relation to that phenomenon which is qualified by this empty nature, and a phenomenon qualified by an empty nature is established in relation to its empty nature. Just as when a phenomenon qualified by an empty nature is analysed it is not found, so too when this phenomenon's empty nature itself is analysed, it is unfindable as well. Therefore, when we seek the object designated as 'an empty nature', this empty nature is also not found. It merely exists through the force of subjective designation done without analysis. Thus it does not inherently exist. The thirteenth chapter of Nāgārjuna's *Fundamental Text Called 'Wisdom'* (XIII. 7–8) says:

> If anything non-empty existed, then
> Something empty would also exist;

> If the non-empty does not exist
> At all, how could the empty do so?
>
> The Conquerors said that emptiness
> Is the remover of all [bad] views;
> Those who view emptiness [as inherently existent]
> Were said to be incurable.

Also, Nāgārjuna's *Praise of the Supramundane* (*Lokātītastava*) says:

> Since the ambrosia of emptiness is taught
> For the sake of forsaking all misconceptions,
> He who adheres to it [as inherently existent]
> Is strongly berated by you [the Buddha].

Therefore, when a tree, for instance, is analysed, the tree is not found, but its mode of being or emptiness is found. Then, when that emptiness is analysed, that emptiness also is not found, but the emptiness of that emptiness is found. This is called an emptiness of an emptiness. Thus, a tree is a conventional truth, and its mode of being is an ultimate truth. Further, when that ultimate truth becomes the basis of analysis and when its mode of being is posited, then that ultimate truth becomes the basis of qualification in relation to the quality that is its mode of being. Thus, there is even an explanation that in these circumstances an emptiness can be viewed as a conventional truth.

Though there are no essential differences among emptinesses, it is said that emptinesses are divided into twenty, eighteen, sixteen, or four types in terms of the bases qualified by emptiness. Briefly, all are included within these two categories: selflessness of persons and selflessness of other phenomena.

Question: How does an emptiness appear to a mind when it ascertains an emptiness?

Answer: If one has a mistaken view of an emptiness, equating it with a vacuity which is a nothingness, this is not the ascertainment of an emptiness. Or, even if one has developed a proper understanding of an emptiness as merely a lack of inherent existence, still, when the vacuity which is a lack of inherent existence appears, one may subsequently lose sight of the original understanding. This vacuity then becomes a mere nothingness with the original understanding of the negation of inherent existence being lost completely. Therefore, this is not the ascertainment of an emptiness either. Also, even if the meaning of an emptiness has been ascertained, but the thought, 'This is an emptiness,' appears, then one is apprehending the existence of an emptiness which is a positive thing. Therefore, that consciousness then becomes a conventional valid cogniser and not the ascertainment of an emptiness. The *Condensed Perfection of Wisdom Sūtra (Sañcayagāthā-prajñāpāramitā)* says, 'Even if a Bodhisattva realises, "These aggregates are empty," he is acting on signs of conventionalities and does not have faith in the state of non-production.'

Further, 'an emptiness' is a negative [an absence] which must be ascertained through the mere elimination of the object of negation, that is, inherent existence. Negatives are of two types: affirming negatives in which some other positive phenomenon is implied in place of the object of negation, and non-affirming negatives in which no other positive phenomenon is implied in place of the object of negation. An emptiness is an instance of the latter; therefore, a consciousness cognising an emptiness necessarily ascertains the mere negative or absence of the object of negation. What appears to the mind is a clear vacuity accompanied by the mere thought, 'These concrete things as they now appear to our minds do not exist at all.' The mere lack of inherent existence or mere truthlessness which is the referent object of this consciousness is an emptiness; therefore, such a mind ascertains an emptiness. Śāntideva's *Engaging in the Bodhisattva Deeds* (IX. 34–35)[4] says:

> When with the thought 'it does not exist' the thing analysed
> Is not apprehended [as inherently existent],
> How could there stand before the mind an [inherently existent]
>   non-thing lacking
> A base [that is, an inherently existent emptiness without the
>   object it qualifies]?
>
> When [inherently existent] things
> And non-things do not stand before the mind,
> Since there is nothing else [inherently existent],
> Then with the intended objects [of the conception
> Of inherent existence] being non-existent, elaborations
> [Of duality and inherent existence] are extinguished.

If an emptiness were not a non-affirming negative but were either an affirming negative implying another phenomenon or a positive phenomenon itself, then a consciousness cognising it would have apprehension [of an inherent existence] or would be involved with signs [of conventionalities]. Thus, the possibility of generating a conceiver of inherent existence would not be eliminated. In that case, the wisdom cognising emptiness would not be the antidote of all conceptions of inherent existence and would be incapable of eliminating the obstructions to enlightenment. Thinking of this, Śāntideva says in his *Engaging in the Bodhisattva Deeds* (IX. 110–111)[5]:

[*Question*]

> When the analyser analysing [whether phenomena inherently
>   exist]
> Analyses [and determines that they are empty of inherent
>   existence],
> Because the analyser also is to be analysed,
> Would it not then be endless?

[*Answer*]

> If the objects of analysis [all phenomena in general]
> Have been analysed [and determined not to exist inherently],
> Then [for that mind] no [further inherently existent] basis
>   [requiring more analysis] exists.
> Because the bases [which are the phenomena qualified by
>   emptiness] do not inherently exist,
> [An object of negation], inherent existence and its negative
> Are not inherently produced, that too is called [the natural]
>   nirvāṇa.[6]

Thus, viewing a base—self, other, and so forth—we ascertain the meaning of its being essentially or naturally at peace, free of inherent existence. If we become familiar with this, the objects viewed—self, other, and so forth—appear as illusion-like or dream-like falsities which, although not inherently existent, appear to be so.

Question: What is the imprint or benefit of such an ascertainment of an emptiness?

Answer: Nāgārjuna's *Fundamental Text Called 'Wisdom'* (XXIV. 18) says:

> That which is dependent-arising
> We explain as emptiness.
> This is dependent imputation;
> Just this is the middle path.

Thus, we understand the natural lack of inherent existence to be the meaning of dependent-arising and understand dependent-arising to be the meaning of the natural lack of inherent existence. Then, we ascertain that emptiness and dependent-arising accompany each other. Through the force of this ascertainment, conventional valid cognisers properly engage in that which is to be adopted and cease doing that which is to be discarded within the context of mere nominal existence. Perverse consciousnesses such as desire, hatred and so forth, generated through the force of adhering to objective existence or non-nominal existence, become gradually weaker and can finally be abandoned.

Let us explain this a little. If the actual experience of the view of emptiness has arisen, we can identify within our experience that whatever objects presently appear to our consciousnesses [eye, ear and so on], they all seem to be inherently existent. We can then know with certainty how the conceiver of inherent existence is generated, and how—at the time of strong attention to these objects—it adheres to the way they appear, and posits them to be true. We will then further know that whatever afflictions are produced, such as desire, hatred, and so forth, a conceiver of inherent existence is acting as their basic cause. Moreover, we will ascertain clearly that this conceiver of inherent existence is a perverse consciousness that is mistaken with respect to its referent object. We will know with certainty how the mode of apprehension of this consciousness lacks a valid foundation. We will also know that its opposite, a consciousness which perceives a selflessness, is a non-perverse consciousness and that its mode of apprehension has the support of valid cognition.

Thus, the glorious Dharmakīrti says in his *Commentary on (Dignāga's) 'Compendium on Valid Cognisers'* (*Pramāṇavārttika*, Chapter I)[7]:

> An ascertaining mind and a falsely superimposing mind
> Are entities of eradicator and that which is eradicated.

And (Chapter I):

> All [defects such as desires] have as their antidote [the wisdom of selflessness]
> In that their decrease and increase depend [on the increase and decrease of that wisdom].
> So through familiarity the mind assumes the nature of
> That wisdom—thus in time the contaminations are extinguished.

A conceiver of inherent existence and a consciousness that has a contradictory mode of apprehension are respectively the eradicated and eradicator. Therefore, it is natural that if one becomes stronger, the other will become weaker. Nāgārjuna's *Praise of the Element of Superior Qualities (Dharmadhātustotra)* says:

> When a metal garment which has become stained with
> Contaminations and is to be cleansed by fire,
> Is put in fire, its stains
> Are burned but it is not,
>
> So, with regard to the mind of clear light
> Which has the stains of desire and so forth,
> Its stains are burned by the fire of wisdom
> But its nature, clear light, is not.

The Conqueror Maitreya's *Sublime Science (Uttaratantra)*[8] says:

> Because the bodies of a perfect Buddha are emanated [to all
>   sentient beings], because reality
> Is not differentiated [since it is the final nature of both Buddhas
>   and sentient beings],
> And because [sentient beings] have the [natural and develop-
>   mental] lineages [suitable
> To develop into a Truth Body and a Form Body],
> Then all embodied beings have the Buddha Nature.

Thus, not only is the ultimate nature of the mind unpolluted by contaminations, but also the conventional nature of the mind, that is, its mere clear knowing, is unpolluted by contaminations as well. Therefore, the mind can become either better or worse, and it is suitable to be transformed. However, no matter how much one cultivates the bad consciousnesses that provide a support for the conception of inherent existence, they cannot be cultivated limitlessly. Cultivation of the good consciousnesses, on the other hand, which are opposite to those and which have the support of valid cognition, can be increased limitlessly. On the basis of this reason, we can ascertain that the stains on the mind can be removed. Thus, the final nature of a mind that has removed its stains so that they will never be generated again is liberation. Therefore, we can become certain that liberation is attainable. Not only that, but just as the contaminations of the afflictions are removable, so are their predispositions as well. Therefore, we can be certain that the final nature of the mind with all the contaminations of the afflictions and their predispositions removed is attainable. This is called a non-abiding nirvāṇa or a Body of Truth. Thereby it is generally established that liberation and omniscience exist.

Nāgārjuna's *Fundamental Text Called 'Wisdom'* (I. Invocation) says:

> I bow down to the perfect Buddha,
> The best of teachers, who propounded
> That what dependently arises
> Has no cessation, no production,
> No annihilation, no permanence, no coming,
> No going, no difference, no sameness,
> Is free of the elaborations [of inherent
> Existence and of duality] and is at peace.

Thus Buddha, the Blessed One, from his own insight taught this dependent-arising as his slogan—showing that because phenomena are dependent-arisings, they have a nature of emptiness, free of the eight extremes of cessation and so forth. If Buddha is thus seen as a reliable being who without error taught definite goodness [liberation and omniscience] along with its means, one will consequently see that the Blessed One was not mistaken even with respect to teaching high status [the pleasures of lives as men and gods] along with its means.

The glorious Dharmakīrti says in his *Commentary on (Dignāga's)* *'Compendium on Valid Cognisers'* (Chapter I)[9]:

> Because [it is established by common inference that Buddha's word] is not mistaken with regard to the principal meaning [the four truths],
> [Due to similarity, Buddha's word] can be inferred [to be not mistaken] with regard to other [extremely obscure subjects as well].

Also, Āryadeva's *Four Hundred* (Chapter XII)[10] says:

> Whoever has generated doubt
> Towards what is not obvious in Buddha's word
> Will believe that only Buddha [is omniscient]
> Based on [his profound teaching of] emptiness.

In brief, through coming to know the Conqueror's scriptures as well as their commentaries, which are all aimed at the achievement of high status and definite goodness, we will attain faith in them. Thereby, induced by valid cognition, we will generate from our hearts faith and respect for the teacher of these scriptures, the Blessed Buddha, and for his followers, the great masters of India. Similarly, we will be able also to generate firm, unchangable faith and respect for the spiritual guides who presently teach us the paths without error and for the Spiritual Community who are our friends abiding properly on the paths on which the Teacher himself travelled. The master Candrakīrti says in his *Seventy Stanzas on the Three Refuges (Triśaraṇasaptati)*[11]:

> The Buddha, his Doctrine and the Supreme Community
> Are the refuges of those wishing liberation.

Thus, we will easily generate certainty that the Three Refuges are the sole source of refuge for those wishing liberation. Those bothered by suffering will go to the Three Excellences for refuge and will generate a firm, indestructible attitude of wishing for liberation, thinking, 'If I could only attain liberation!' Similarly, having understood the suffering condition of all other sentient beings from our own experience of suffering, we will generate the wish to establish them as well in liberation, that is, in emancipation from suffering, and in omniscience. For the sake of accomplishing this, an extremely steady and very powerful aspiration to enlightenment, wishing to attain enlightenment ourselves, will be produced, and the ability to generate this attitude will arise.

If our motivation is that of a Hīnayānist, working only for our own release from cyclic existence, our progress is as follows. First, we establish as our foundation any of the forms of ethics for householders or monks. Then with this foundation as our base, when we are on the path of accumulation, we familiarise ourselves again and again with the subtle, deep and very meaningful view of emptiness explained above through hearing and thinking about it. Thereby, our viewing consciousness gradually develops into the wisdom which arises from meditation and which is the union of calm abiding and special insight cognising an emptiness conceptually. In this way, the path of preparation is attained. Then, gradually we attain the path of seeing, a true path, a jewel of doctrine, perceiving emptiness directly. [Thus paths in this context are states of consciousness leading to a nirvāṇa, and] through the path of seeing acting as an antidote, we begin to attain true cessations of suffering. These true cessations are states of having utterly abandoned forever both true sources of suffering, such as intellectually acquired conceptions of inherent existence, as well as true sufferings, such as rebirths in bad migrations. That which is abandoned in both cases follows a progression of increasing refinement. Thus, through the path of meditation, which is a further familiarisation with the truth, i.e., emptiness, already seen, we attain step by step the true cessations, which are states of having utterly abandoned forever the innate afflictions, again beginning with the gross ones. Finally, when we attain liberation, which is the state of having abandoned the subtlest of the small afflictions together with their seeds, the travelling of our own path [as a Hīnayānist] has finished. Thus is realised the stage of no more learning, a position reached in the Hīnayāna by a Foe Destroyer [or *arhan*, the chief enemy being the conception of inherent existence].

When our motivation is to attain highest enlightenment for the sake of all sentient beings, the wisdoms of hearing, thinking, and meditating, directed towards the meaning of emptiness, are generated in such a way that they are accompanied by the skilful means of the perfections [giving, ethics, patience, effort, concentration, and wisdom], which arise from this Mahāyāna motivation. The view becomes more and more profound, and when emptiness is cognised directly, the path of seeing, and simultaneously the wisdom of the first stage of the Mahāyāna, are both attained. The first of the accumulations of wisdom and merit, which takes one countless aeon [begun on the path of accumulation], is thus completed. As was previously explained, we then begin to realise the true cessations, which are states of having utterly abandoned forever the intellectually acquired conceptions of inherent existence and so on. Then, during the seven impure Bodhisattva stages, the accumulations of merit and wisdom are amassed over a second countless aeon. During the three pure stages we begin the gradual abandonment of the obstructions to simultaneous cognition of all objects of knowledge. These obstructions are the predispositions that have been established by the conception of inherent existence and the subtle bad habits produced by them. When the third accumulation over a countless aeon is completed, a Body of Truth, a true cessation, which is the state of having utterly abandoned forever all types of defects, is attained. The Three Bodies of Truth, Complete Enjoyment, and Emanation are simultaneously manifested, and the position of Buddhahood, which is the perfection of wisdom, love, and power, is realised.

Moreover, if we have trained our mental continuum well by means of:

1 the thought definitely to leave cyclic existence,
2 the altruistic aspiration to highest enlightenment, and
3 the correct view of emptiness,

and, in addition, have the fortune of having completed well
the causal collections of both merit and wisdom [then we are
qualified to enter the tantric path]. If from among the quick
paths of Secret Mantra we advance through any of the paths
of the three lower tantras, we will become enlightened more
quickly [than had we followed the sūtra paths alone]. Enlightenment is speedily attained through the power of special
means for achieving a Form Body and through the quick
achievement of the yoga of the union of calm abiding and
special insight, and so forth. Further, on the path of the fourth
and highest tantra we learn, in addition to the former practices,
to differentiate the coarse, subtle, and extremely subtle winds
[energies] and consciousnesses. The extremely subtle mental
consciousness itself is generated into the entity of a path
consciousness, and through cultivating it, the consciousness
cognising emptiness becomes extremely powerful. Thus, the
highest tantra has the distinguishing feature of making the
abandonment of obstructions extremely swift.

Let us speak briefly about how to internalise the view of
emptiness. Meditation on the view of emptiness is done for the
sake of abandoning obstructions; therefore, a vast collection
of merit is needed. Further, to amass such through the rite of
the seven branches encompasses much and has great purpose.
The seven branches are prostrating, offering, revealing our
own faults, admiring our own and others' virtues, petitioning
the Buddhas to teach, entreating the Buddhas to remain in the
world, and dedicating the merit of such to all sentient beings.
With regard to the field for amassing the collection of merit,
it is permissible to do whatever suits our own inclinations,
either directing our mind towards the actual Three Excellences
in general or towards any particular object of refuge that is

visualised in front of ourselves. [For this see the *Precious Garland*, 466–85 in volume 2 of this series.]

Then, after we petition the refuges for help in generating the view of emptiness in our continuum, the way to conduct the actual meditation session is as follows. If initially we meditate on the selflessness of the person, it is said to be easier for meditation, because the subject [is continually present]. Therefore, we should ascertain well how the meditator appears to our mind in the thought, 'Now I am meditating on the view of emptiness.' We should ascertain well how the 'I' appears to the mind when the 'I' experiences pleasure or pain. We should also ascertain well the mode of the adherence to the 'I'. Based on that, we should analyse the way the 'I' exists as was explained above. Gradually our understanding and experience of the view of emptiness becomes more profound, and when we engage in analysis at that point, the thought will arise, 'The independent mode of appearance of the "I", such as previously appeared, is utterly non-existent.' At that time, we should set our mind single-pointedly for a period of time on just that clear vacuity which is the mere negative of the object of negation and then perform stabilising meditation without analysis. If our mind's mode of apprehension of this clear vacuity of the negation loosens slightly [and this vacuity starts to become a mere nothingness], then we should again perform analytical meditation on the 'I' as before. Alternately sustaining analytical and stabilising meditation thus serves as a means of transforming the mind.

If through having analysed the 'I' a little understanding of emptiness arises, we should then analyse the mental and physical aggregates in dependence on which the 'I' is imputed. It is very important to analyse well the aggregates of forms, feelings, discriminations, compositional factors, and consciousnesses in general and the aggregate of consciousnesses in particular. Further, it is in general difficult to identify even the conventional mode of being of the mind. Once the conventional

87

nature of the mind—the mere clear knower—has been identified, then, through analysing its nature, finally we will gradually be able to identify the ultimate nature of the mind. If that is done, there is great progress unlike anything else.

At the beginning we should meditate for half an hour. When we rise from the session and various good and bad objects appear, benefit and harm are manifestly experienced. Therefore, we should develop as much as we can the realisation that these phenomena do not exist objectively and are mere dependent-arisings of appearances, like illusions [in that they only seem to be inherently existent].

We should meditate in this way in four formal sessions: at sunrise, in the morning, afternoon, and evening. Or, if possible, we should meditate in six or eight or more sessions, scheduling them at equal intervals throughout the day and night. If this is not possible, we should meditate in only two sessions, in the morning and the evening. When our understanding and experience of the view of emptiness become a little stronger, ascertainment of the view will arise spontaneously during all activities, when we are going, wandering, sleeping, or staying. Also, since without a calm abiding directed toward an emptiness there is no chance for generating a special insight that cognises an emptiness, it is definitely necessary to seek a calm abiding. Therefore, we should learn its methods from other books.

If we do not wish merely to know intellectually about the view of emptiness, but rather wish to experience it ourselves in our own continuum, we should build a firm foundation for this through what has been explained above. Then, according to our mental ability we should hear and consider both the sūtras and treatises which teach the profound view of emptiness as well as the good explanations of them by the experienced Tibetan scholars in their commentaries. Together with this, we should learn to make our own ways of generating experience of emptiness accord with the precepts of an experienced wise man.

> Through the collections of virtues arising from my effort here
> May all sentient beings wishing happiness, myself and others,
> Attain the eye which sees reality, free of extremes,
> And proceed to the land of enlightenment.

This has been written for the sake of helping in general those with burgeoning intellect in the East and West and in particular those who, though they wish to know the very profound and subtle meaning of emptiness or selflessness, either do not have the opportunity to study the great Mādhyamika books or cannot read and understand the treatises existing in the Tibetan language. Thus, it has been written mainly with the intent of easy comprehension and for the sake of easy translation into other languages. May this which has been written by the Buddhist monk, Tenzin Gyatso, bring virtuous goodness.

Notes

Except where noted, all editions are those in the rNam-rgyal Grva-tshang Library in Dharamsala. For the titles of the commentaries see the Bibliography.

1 The *Fundamental Text Called 'Wisdom'* and the *Treatise on the Middle Way* are the same book. This and the next quote are translated in accordance with Tsong-ka-pa's commentary.

2 The parenthetical additions are from Tsong-ka-pa's commentary: Tokyo-Kyoto ed., vol 154 49-1-1 through 51-1-7.

3 Ignorance, action, consciousness, name and form, six sources, contact, feeling, attachment, grasping, existence, birth, and ageing and death.

4 Parenthetical additions are from Gyel-tsap's (rGyal-tshab) commentary, 127a.2 through 127a.5.

5 Parenthetical additions are from Gyel-tsap's commentary, 145a.1 through 145b.2.

6 According to Gyel-tsap: That absence of inherent existence is said to be the natural nirvāṇa of all phenomena. Or, another meaning of the line, also according to Gyel-tsap: Through realising and meditating on the meaning of non-inherent existence it is said that nirvāṇa is attained.

7 Parenthetical additions to the second quote are from Kay-drup's (mKhas-grub) commentary, 134b.3-4.

8 Parenthetical additions are from Gyel-tsap's commentary, 73b.5 through 74a.2.

9 Parenthetical additions are from Kay-drup's commentary, 135b.6-7.

10 Parenthetical additions are from Gyel-tsap's commentary, 90b.3 through 91a.3.

11 Page 279b.4, volume khi of the sNar-thang bsTan-'gyur in the Library of Tibetan Works and Archives, Dharamsala.

Bibliography

The number of the texts and volumes in the Suzuki Research Foundation publication of the Peking edition are given after the Sanskrit and Tibetan titles.

I TEXTS QUOTED BY THE AUTHOR

Commentary on (Dignāga's) 'Compendium on Valid Cognisers' by Dharmakīrti
Pramāṇavārttika
Tshad ma rnam 'grel
(P5709, vol 130)
Condensed Perfection of Wisdom Sūtra by Buddha
Sañcayagāthā-prajñāpāramitā-sūtra
Shes rab kyi pha rol tu phyin pa sdud pa tshigs su bcad pa
(P735, vol 21)
Engaging in the Bodhisattva Deeds by Śāntideva
Bodhicaryāvatāra
Byang chub sems dpa'i spyod pa la 'jug pa
(P5272, vol 99)
Four Hundred or *Treatise of Four Hundred Stanzas* by Āryadeva
Catuḥśatakaśāstrakārikā
bsTan bcos bzhi brgya pa zhes bya ba'i tshig le'ur byas pa
(P5246, vol 95)
Fundamental Text Called 'Wisdom' or *Fundamental Stanzas on the Middle Way Called 'Wisdom'* by Nāgārjuna
Prajñā-nāma-mūlamadhyamakakārikā
dBu ma rtsa ba'i tshig le'ur byas pa shes rab ces bya ba
(P5224, vol 95)
Hundred Thousand Stanza Perfection of Wisdom Sūtra by Buddha
Śatasāhasrikā-prajñāpāramitā-sūtra
Shes rab kyi pha rol tu phyin pa stong phrag brgya pa
(P730, vol 12–18)
Kāśyapa Chapter in the *Pile of Jewels Sūtra* by Buddha
Kāśyapaparivarta-sūtra [in the] Ratnakūṭa-sūtra
'Od srung gi le'u'i mdo [in the] dKon mchog brtseg pa'i mdo
(P760–43, vol 24)

91

Ornament of the Mahāyāna Sūtras by Maitreya
Mahāyānasūtrālaṃkāra
Theg pa chen po'i mdo sde'i rgyan
(P5521, vol 108)

Praise of the Element of Superior Qualities by Nāgārjuna
Dharmadhātustotra
Chos kyi dbyings su bstod pa
(P2010, vol 46)

Praise of the Supramundane by Nāgārjuna
Lokātītastava
'Jig rten las 'das par bstod pa
(P2012, vol 46)

Precious Garland of Advice for the King by Nāgārjuna
Rājaparikathāratnāvalī
rGyal po la gtam bya ba rin po che'i phreng ba
(P5658, vol 129)

Questions of the King of Nāgas, Anavatapta, Sūtra by Buddha
Anavataptanāgarājaparipṛcchā-sūtra
Klu'i rgyal po ma dros pas zhus pa'i mdo
(P823, vol 33)

Seventy Stanzas on Emptiness by Nāgārjuna
Śūnyatāsaptatikārikā
sTong pa nyid bdun cu pa'i tshig le'ur byas pa
(P5227, vol 95)

Seventy Stanzas on the Three Refuges by Candrakīrti
Triśaraṇasaptati
gSum la skyabs su 'gro ba bdun cu pa
(P5366, vol 103)

Sublime Science or *Mahāyāna Treatise on the Sublime Science* by Maitreya
Mahāyānottaratantraśāstra
Theg pa chen po rgyud bla ma'i bstan bcos
(P5525, vol. 108)

Supplement to (Nāgārjuna's) 'Treatise on the Middle Way' by Candrakīrti
Madhyamakāvatāra
dBu ma la 'jug pa
(P5262, vol 98)

Sūtra on the Four Truths by Buddha
Catuḥsatya-sūtra
bDen pa bzhi'i mdo
(P982, vol 39)

Twenty-Five Thousand Stanza Perfection of Wisdom Sūtra by Buddha
Pañcaviṃśatisāhasrikā-prajñāpāramitā-sūtra
Shes rab kyi pha rol tu phyin pa stong phrag nyi shu lnga pa
(P731, vol 18–19)
Unravelling of the Thought Sūtra by Buddha
Saṃdhinirmocana-sūtra
dGongs pa nges par 'grel pa'i mdo
P774, vol 29)

II COMMENTARIES CITED BY THE TRANSLATORS

*Brilliant Illumination of the Thought, An Explanation of (Candrakīrti's)
Treatise 'Supplement to (Nāgārjuna's) "Fundamental Treatise on the
Middle Way"'* by Tsong-ka-pa (Tsong-kha-pa)
bsTan bcos chen po dbu ma la 'jug pa'i rnam bshad dgongs pa rab gsal
(P6143, vol 154)
Commentary on (Maitreya's) 'Mahāyāna Treatise on the Sublime Science'
by Gyel-tsap (rGyal-tshab)
Theg pa chen po rgyud bla ma'i ṭīkā
*Entrance of the Buddha Sons, An Explanation of (Śāntideva's) 'Engaging
in the Bodhisattva Deeds'* by Gyel-tsap (rGyal-tshab)
Byang chub sems dpa'i spyod pa la 'jug pa'i rnam bshad rgyal sras
'jug ngogs
*Essence of the Good Expositions, An Explanation of (Āryadeva's) 'Four
Hundred'* by Gyel-tsap (rGyal-tshab)
bZhi brgya pa'i rnam bshad legs bshad snying po
*Ocean of Reasoning, An Extensive Explanation of the Great Treatise
(Dharmakīrti's) 'Commentary on (Dignāga's) "Compendium on Valid
Cognisers"'* by Kay-drup (mKhas-grub)
rGyas pa'i bstan bcos tshad ma rnam 'grel gyi rgya cher bshad pa rigs
pa'i rgya mtsho

93

Glossary

Abhidharma: Knowledge, the study of phenomena
Adhiprajñā: Higher wisdom
Adhisamādhi: Higher meditative stabilisation
Adhiśīla: Higher ethics
Anuttara-yoga: Highest Yoga, the fourth of the four sets of tantras
Arhan: Foe Destroyer
Ārya: Superior
Āryan: Superior, a person who has become elevated over common beings
    through directly cognising emptiness
Āyatana: Sources
Caryā: Performance, the second of the four sets of tantras
Dharma: That which holds, phenomenon, religious practice
Dharma-kāya: Truth Body, Body of Wisdom and of Nirvāṇa
Dhātu: Types
Hīnayāna: Lesser Vehicle
Kriyā: Action, the first of the four sets of tantras
Mahāyāna: Great Vehicle
Nirmāṇakāya: Emanation Body
Prajñā: Wisdom
Pratyekabuddha: Solitary Realiser
Rūpa-kāya: Form Body
Samādhi: Meditative stabilisation
Śamatha: Calm abiding
Śīla: Ethics
Skandha: Mental and physical aggregates
Śrāvaka: Hearer
Sūtrānta: Class of scripture
Tīrthika: Forder, a non-Buddhist propounding a ford or passage to
    liberation.
Triśikṣā: Three trainings
Vinaya: Discipline
Vipaśyanā: Special insight

Index